Writing from Ireland

THE CENTRAL SCHOOL OF SPEECH AND DRAMA

UNIVERSITY OF LONDON

Please return or renew this item by the last date shown.

The Library, Central School of Speech and Drama,
Embassy Theatre, Eton Avenue, London, NW3 3HY
http://heritage.cssd.ac.uk
library@cssd.ac.uk
Direct line: 0207 559 3942

Figures in a Landscape

Writing from Australia edited by Wendy Morgan
Writing from Canada edited by Jim Rice and Mike Hayhoe
Writing from India edited by Lakshmi Holmström and Mike Hayhoe
Writing from Ireland edited by Valerie Quinlivan
Writing from South Africa edited by Anthony Adams and Ken Durham

Figures in a Landscape

Writing from Ireland

Valerie Quinlivan

CAMBRIDGE
UNIVERSITY PRESS

Published by the Press Syndicate of the University of Cambridge

The Pitt Building, Trumpington Street, Cambridge CB2 1RP

40 West 20th Street, New York, NY 1001-4211, USA

10 Stamford Road, Oakleigh, Melbourne 3166, Australia

First published 1995

Printed in Great Britain at the University Press, Cambridge

A catalogue record for this book is available from the British Library

ISBN 0 521 439957 paperback

Notice to teachers

Cover illustration: HarperCollins Publishers/Douglas Robertson

Contents

Acknowledgements   *page* vi

Introduction   ix

Map of Ireland   xv

Three Lambs   Liam O'Flaherty   1
First Fish   Aisling Maguire   5
The Trout   Seán O'Faoláin   11
First Confession   Frank O'Connor   15
The Half-Crown   James Plunkett   23
The Story of the Widow's Son   Mary Lavin   35
The Rug   Edna O'Brien   47
Mr Sing My Heart's Delight   Brian Friel   55
All Fall Down   Helen Lucy Burke   65
The Wrong Vocation   Moy McCrory   73
Feet   Seamus Deane   85
The Year 1912   Máirtín Ó Cadhain*   90
Village Without Men   Margaret Barrington   103
Floodtide   Máirtín Ó Cadhain*   115
The Passing of Billy Condit   Sam McAughtry   127
The Talker   Seán Lucy   139
The Sniper   Liam O'Flaherty   149
The Wall Reader   Fiona Barr   153
Oranges from Spain   David Park   161
Belfast Woman   Mary Beckett   174

Glossary   186

translated by Eoghan ÓTuairisc

Acknowledgements

I would like to thank the state schools who expressed enthusiasm for this project and who managed to trial single stories in their classrooms. My gratitude for extensive cooperation also goes to teachers and students of The International School of Brussels, Marymount School, Rome, The International School of Milan and the Vienna International School as well as St Andrew's College, Dublin, and my own students at the United World College of the Adriatic. My thanks are also due to Stella Quinlivan for her help in finding material inaccessible to me when I was in Italy, to Patrick Quinlivan for his historical expertise and to Mike Hayhoe for his continuing support. The National Gallery of Ireland, the Municipal Gallery, Dublin, and in particular the Irish Arts Council have been valuable sources for illustrations.

Thanks are due to the following for permission to reproduce illustrations: p. xvi Liam White Photography; p.6 Bill Doyle; p.10 National Gallery of Ireland; p.24 Steve Jansen, Life File; p.36 Courtesy of Martin Gale; p.54 Fr. F.M. Browne, SJ Collection; p.66 Herbert Art Gallery & Museum, Coventry; p.72 National Gallery of Ireland; p.84 Joan Wakelin, Trip; p.102 Courtesy of Dermot McCarthy; p.114 Liam White Photography; p.126 The Hogg Collection, Ulster Museum, Belfast; p.138 Crawford Municipal Art Gallery, Cork; p.154 Courtesy of Dermot Seymour.

Thanks are due to the following for permission to reproduce stories: p.1 'Three Lambs' by Liam O'Flaherty from *Spring Sowing*, reprinted by permission of the Peters Fraser and Dunlop Group Limited; p.5 'First Fish' by Aisling Maguire © Aisling Maguire; p.11 'The Trout' by Seán O'Faoláin, reproduced by permission of Rogers, Coleridge and White Limited; p.15 'First Confession' by Frank O'Connor from *My Oedipus Complex and Other Stories*, reprinted by permission of Peters Fraser and Dunlop Group Limited; p.23 'The Half Crown' by James Plunkett, reprinted by permission of the Peters Fraser and Dunlop Group Limited; p.35 'The Story of the Widow's Son' by Mary Lavin from *The Stories of Mary Lavin*, reprinted by permission of Constable Publishers; p.47 'The Rug' by Edna O'Brien, from *The Love Object*, reprinted by permission of A.M. Heath and Company Limited; p.55 'Mr Sing My Heart's Delight' by Brian Friel – © Brian Friel, 1959, repro-

Introduction

Like most people with Irish backgrounds, I draw on two cultures, the Irish and the English, since they have been inextricably mingled for centuries; also for me, as for the majority of Irish nowadays, the European dimension is very important, both culturally and economically. Some contemporary Irish writers have moved away from their roots altogether but the majority, especially short-story writers, still deal with specifically Irish topics or the tangled relationships of emigrant Irish with their homeland. For this reason it is important to understand something of the cultural and historic background to enjoy the stories in this book.

Ireland is an island on the extreme west of Europe. You can stand on its western cliffs and look over the wild Atlantic that stretches for 2,000 miles to America. From its eastern coast the ferries ply the mere 60 miles or so across the Irish Sea to Ireland's nearest neighbour, Britain. Despite their proximity to this once-great colonising power, Irish people have remained distinct and recognisable by their names, accents and culture.

Everywhere you go in the world the Irish seem known, not only because of the media-borne violence from Northern Ireland but also because of their songs and music; because some traveller has left a mark on history or because there's 'a touch of Irish' in the family.

Centuries before Christopher Columbus, the Irish Saint Brendan gave storytellers something to sing about by sailing to America. The Irish have been made local heroes in many a country: Bouchier in Bulgaria, De Lacy in Russia, O'Donnell in Spain and O'Higgins in Chile, MacMahon in France and the suffragette Kate Shepherd in New Zealand. Heroes apart, I found more of my own namesakes in New Zealand than there are in Ireland and I have met cousins in my travels on four continents.

The Irish have a great reputation as storytellers. Until recently the *seanchai*, or professional storyteller, was a popular figure in rural Ireland. His tales could be of familiar happenings or drawn from the far distant past. More than 2,000 years ago the Celtic peoples displaced the original Stone Age inhabitants and overran the circular earth forts and the massive underground galleries and graves, some of which had already been standing for four thousand years. The Celts brought with them an advanced culture. They established the four kingdoms – now provinces – of Ulster, Leinster, Munster and Connacht, with a High King over all. In the 5th century AD, with the coming of the missionary, Saint Patrick, they converted to Christianity and their language was influenced by the Latin of the scholar-monks; some left Ireland to establish monastic centres of learning throughout Europe.

In the 12th century, the Norman-French, rulers of England, invaded Ireland; the King of England was proclaimed Lord of Ireland, although the Irish kings remained in power. Many of these Normans became totally integrated with the Irish, adopting their language and customs. In the 16th century, Queen Elizabeth I sent armies to subdue 'the troublesome Irish' and granted Irish land as gifts to her lords and soldiers. Many of these colonialists also became absorbed by the culture, even adopting the outlawed religion, Catholicism.

It was really in the beginning of the next century, the 17th, that Ireland's 'troubles' began in earnest. Land grants continued on a huge scale and peasants and landowners were driven from their homes. Those who were not slaughtered for resisting were driven to the infertile province of Connacht. Over 100,000 Lowland Scots were shipped to the northern province of Ulster to take their place. The risings which followed resulted in the massacre of thousands of these Scots. This period established the antagonisms which still persist in the North. Cromwell and his Puritan followers were determined to suppress the Irish and their Catholic religion. He crushed rebellion savagely and established leaders of the immigrant population in the North as rulers there. A later rising, supported by the deposed Stuart monarchy, was defeated by Prince William of Orange, later William III of England, in 1690. Pictures of 'King Billy' still adorn 'loyalist' standards in the North. Loyalty to the British crown and the Protestant religion mark the solidarity of many Irish of Ulster Scots origin today.

Throughout the next two centuries the Catholic Irish fared no better. Laws denied them the right to their religion, language, education and land. In order to survive they had to master English and gradually the old Irish language of the Celts was supplanted. The mid-19th-century famine, when the staple diet of potatoes failed and other crops were exported, brought the Irish to their lowest ebb and halved the population from eight to four million. Many of the famine survivors left the country, mainly to go to America.

They journeyed from their small farms and villages, often for the first time, with little English and barely the passage money for the ship. Many of them left their families, promising to send what money they could from the rich land of America. Songs and stories of the time speak of the sadness of leaving and the excitement and dreams of good fortune and riches. Most endured poverty and ill-health in the unfamiliar world of some big city, and years of hard work struggling to send the passage money to the next brother or sister. If they did return to Ireland from life in an alien land, they had to adapt anew to the ways of life of their childhood.

But nostalgic songs, picture-postcard beauty and even media-portrayed violence, do not give a realistic picture of modern Ireland. The beauty exists in both North and South; the violence exists also, most obviously in the North, particularly in Belfast. It can be a confusing picture. Even the references to 'North' and 'South', and the name 'Ireland' itself, are ambiguous. The ambiguity lies in the fact that the county of Donegal in the Republic of Ireland lies further north than Northern Ireland and the historical province of Ulster stretches beyond the confines of British-ruled Ulster.

I have taken the most common usages, although they would be challenged by some people: 'Ireland' refers to the whole island. Lower-case letters refer to geographic areas: the south, northern, in the west, etc. Upper-case letters refer to politically defined areas: Northern Ireland, the South, etc. The former is often referred to as Ulster and the latter as the Republic.

In the eyes of some there has been an occupying force in Ireland for 800 years. In England's oldest colony the last insurrection began with the 1916 Easter Rising in Dublin. Nineteenth-century revolutionary groups had laid the basis of the Irish Republican Army (IRA), illegal in British times and still illegal in both South and North now. From the beginning of this century the political party, Sinn Fein (By Ourselves), was committed to Irish independence from Britain. From 1919 to 1921 the IRA waged a guerrilla war for the same aim. The treaty which ended this war resulted in 26 of the 32 counties of Ireland becoming the Irish Free State in 1922 and the Republic of Ireland in 1949. Six counties in the north, with Belfast the main city and much of the population of Scottish descent, remained part of the United Kingdom. This is the region which is now referred to as Northern Ireland or Ulster.

In 1968 a campaign for civil rights by the Catholic population of the North led to open conflict. This resulted in a heavier presence of British troops and the eventual emergence of a Provisional Irish Republican Army. This new IRA has carried war for a united Ireland outside the boundaries of the country and across the world. When bombs explode in England the public is reminded of the Ulster problem and the old labels hit the headlines again: Republicans versus Unionists; Catholics versus Protestants. Economics, politics and religion all play their part in the continuing struggle.

Many of the stories in this book have religion as their focus, for in both parts of Ireland religion is a strong element in people's lives. In the North, Catholicism and Protestantism coexist, often peacefully, sometimes in mutual suspicion or even hatred, for it suits extremists of the outlawed military groups of both sides to keep this hatred alive.

In the Republic, 95 per cent of the population is Catholic and most of these go to church regularly. Many are educated in schools run by religious orders of nuns, monks or priests, as are Northern Catholics. It is normal that family life is marked by a series of steps denoting growth within the religious faith. Baptism welcomes the new baby into the church community. At about seven years children make their First Confessions, showing awareness of the difference between good and bad actions and as acts of preparation; this is because, shortly afterwards, they will receive First Communion, the consecrated bread, in company with their family and most of the churchgoers of the parish.

This is an involvement which for many people will continue all their lives. Young adolescents confirm their faith in public and are blessed by a bishop at Confirmation. These occasions, like marriage, are marked by celebration, new clothes and parties as well as by prayer. Death is regarded as part of this cycle. In spite of modern society's alienation from death elsewhere, in Ireland the dead often lie at home before burial and the bereaved family are visited by relations and neighbours; this ceremony – or 'wake', as it is called – can include music and stories and celebration of the life of the person who has died.

The Catholic Irish are usually familiar and easy with their religion. They often have pictures and statues in their houses connected with their faith. Conversation, especially among older people, can naturally include phrases and words with religious connotation – 'It's a fine day, thanks be to God', 'I'll go on my holidays, God willing', 'My old auntie died the other day, God be with her'. It may seem strange, also, that 'Catholic' cultures such as Ireland, Spain or Italy often use such names as 'Jesus' or 'Christ' familiarly or even as expletives in their speech, in a way shocking to other Christian societies. Religion in Ireland can also be felt as an oppressive force, too all-encompassing. Many works of Irish literature deal with the attempt to escape its powerful childhood influence.

All the stories in this collection are in English, although two are translated from Irish. English is spoken by everyone in Ireland, but many people study Irish at school and some are bilingual; this is true of some schools and universities in the North as well as in the South. In the Republic some official documents are in Irish (my birth certificate, for example). Few people speak Irish as a mother tongue any more, however, and some families have not spoken it for generations; yet the old Irish language has shaped the usage of English in Ireland. It may be in the order of words: instead of, 'Are you going to the shops?', you may hear, 'Is it to the shops you are going?'. Or it may be a different way of using parts of speech, such as, 'Look at herself standing there, as bold as you please!' Or it may be the use of Irish words in English and other languages: brogue, shanty, pillion, slogan, smidgin or slob, for example; and words with historic links such as the verb, 'to boycott'.

There has been a written literature in Ireland for 1,500 years, the third oldest in Europe after Greek and Latin. From far further back than that there has been a tradition of spoken or sung poetry and storytelling. The old stories of heroes and battles and romance were handed down from one generation to another by the professional travelling singers or by people by their fires in the dark winters. This oral tradition still exists and stories are begun and embroidered in pubs, at bus stops and across garden fences, with a wealth of expression and vivid imagery worthy of a *seanchai*.

Ireland is still a rural country, although many old farms are abandoned and most of the western isles, where fishing was the livelihood, are now uninhabited. Yet the tourist can still find the meadows and mountains of sentimental ballads sloping down to the sea. The Irish people you meet are likely to be friendly and talkative. In this respect Ireland has not changed. But Ireland, North and South, is part of modern Europe with trade contacts all over the world. The mid-western part, with its countryside and broad Shannon River, also has a busy international airport and a mosque. Local airports speed up business; for some, this allows commuting to replace emigration! Dublin and Belfast are busy capitals where business people, students and visitors come from all over the world. Irish music groups and films win international renown while Irish poems, novels and stories have long been acclaimed.

The stories in this book have been chosen from the past 70 years. Some things have not changed in that time and some have changed with the rest of Europe. Most farmhouses have central heating now, ultra-modern bathrooms and television, and even the provincial cities are more congested; but there are still children who help lambs to be born. Modern life has not stopped alcoholism and, sadly, drugs and Aids have come to Ireland too. Religion is not quite the force it used to be but it weaves a rhythm through most people's lives. In the North it is still sometimes drummed through the streets, to rouse violence and counter-violence. Ireland continues to be a major presence in British politics.

Each of the figures in these stories moves through a personal and national landscape. I hope they draw you in with them to give you some understanding of Ireland, its history, its present and its people.

Valerie Quinlivan

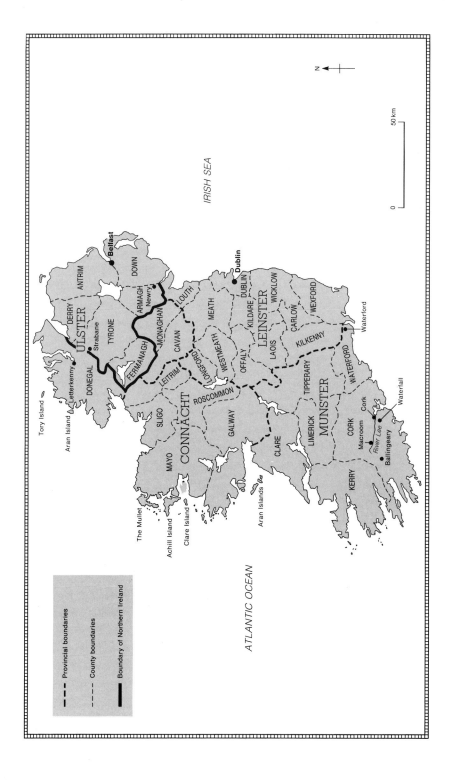

In County Wicklow

Three Lambs

LIAM O'FLAHERTY 1924

Although this is the oldest of the tales in the book, it has not really dated. Even today the majority of Irish children live in the country and know the rural ways of life. Everyday economics must often outweigh the wonders of nature. In this simple story a young boy shows he is familiar with birth and yet to him it is still a source of mystery and total delight.

Little Michael rose before dawn. He tried to make as little noise as possible. He ate two slices of bread and butter and drank a cup of milk, although he hated cold milk with bread and butter in the morning. But on an occasion like this, what did it matter what a boy ate? He was going out to watch the black sheep having a lamb. His father had mentioned the night before that the black sheep was sure to lamb that morning, and of course there was a prize, three pancakes, for the first one who saw the lamb.

He lifted the latch gently and stole out. It was best not to let his brother John know he was going. He would be sure to want to come too. As he ran down the lane, his sleeves, brushing against the evergreen bushes, were wetted by the dew, and the tip of his cap was just visible above the hedge, bobbing up and down as he ran. He was in too great a hurry to open the gate and tore a little hole in the breast of his blue jersey climbing over it. But he didn't mind that. He would get another one on his thirteenth birthday.

He turned to the left from the main road, up a lane that led to the field where his father, the magistrate, kept his prize sheep. It was only a quarter of a mile, that lane, but he thought that it would never end and he kept tripping among the stones that strewed the road. It was so awkward to run on the stones wearing shoes, and it was too early in the year yet to be allowed to go barefooted. He envied Little Jimmy, the son of the farm labourer, who was allowed to go barefooted all the year round, even in the depths of winter, and who always had such wonderful cuts on his big toes, the envy of all the little boys in the village school.

He climbed over the fence leading into the fields and, clapping his hands together, said 'Oh, you devil,' a swear word he had learned from Little Jimmy and of which he was very proud. He took off his shoes and stockings and hid them in a hole in the fence. Then he ran jumping, his bare heels looking like brown spots as he tossed them up behind him. The grass was wet and the ground was hard, but he persuaded himself that it was great fun.

Going through a gap into the next field, he saw a rabbit nibbling grass. He halted suddenly, his heart beating loudly. Pity he hadn't a dog. The rabbit stopped eating. He cocked up his ears. He stood on his tail, with his neck craned up and his forefeet hanging limp. Then he came down again. He thrust his ears forward. Then he lay flat with his ears buried in his back and lay still. With a great yell Little Michael darted forward imitating a dog barking and the rabbit scurried away in short sharp leaps. Only his white tail was visible in the grey light.

Little Michael went into the next field, but the sheep were nowhere to be seen. He stood on a hillock and called out 'Chowin, chowin,' three times. Then he heard 'Mah-m-m-m' in the next field and ran on. The sheep were in the last two fields, two oblong little fields, running in a hollow between two crags, surrounded by high thick fences, the walls of an old fort. In the nearest of the two fields he found ten of the sheep, standing side by side, looking at him, with their fifteen lambs in front of them also looking at him curiously. He counted them out loud and then he saw that the black sheep was not there. He panted with excitement. Perhaps she already had a lamb in the next field. He hurried to the gap leading into the next field, walking stealthily, avoiding the spots where the grass was high, so as to make less noise. It was bad to disturb a sheep that was lambing. He peered through a hole in the fence and could see nothing. Then he crawled to the gap and peered around the corner. The black sheep was just inside standing with her forefeet on a little mound.

Her belly was swollen out until it ended on each side in a sharp point and her legs appeared to be incapable of supporting her body. She turned her head sharply and listened. Little Michael held his breath, afraid to make a noise. It was of vital importance not to disturb the sheep. Straining back to lie down he burst a button on his trousers and he knew his braces were undone. He said, 'Oh, you devil,' again and decided to ask his mother to let him wear a belt instead of braces, same as Little Jimmy wore. Then he crawled farther back from the gap and taking off his braces altogether made it into a belt. It hurt his hips, but he felt far better and manly.

Then he came back again to the gap and looked. The black sheep was still in the same place. She was scratching the earth with her forefeet and going around in a circle, as if she wanted to lie down but was afraid to lie down. Sometimes she ground her teeth and made an awful noise, baring her jaws and turning her head around sideways. Little Michael felt a pain in his heart in pity for her, and he wondered why the other sheep didn't come to keep her company. Then he wondered whether his mother had felt the same pain when she had Ethna the autumn before. She must have, because the doctor was there.

Suddenly the black sheep went on her knees. She stayed a few seconds on her knees and then she moaned and sank to the ground and stretched herself out with her neck on the little hillock and her hindquarters falling down the little slope. Little Michael forgot about the pain now. His heart thumped with excitement. He forgot to breathe, looking intently. 'Ah,' he said. The sheep stretched again and struggled to her feet and circled around once, stamping and grinding her teeth. Little Michael moved up to her slowly. She looked at him anxiously, but she was too sick to move away. He broke the bladder and he saw two little feet sticking out. He seized them carefully and pulled. The sheep moaned again and pressed with all her might. The lamb dropped on the grass.

Little Michael sighed with delight and began to rub its body with his finger-nails furiously. The sheep turned around and smelt it, making a funny happy noise in its throat. The lamb, its white body covered with yellow slime, began to move, and presently it tried to stand up, but it fell again and Little Michael kept rubbing it, sticking his fingers into its ears and nostrils to clear them. He was so intent on this work that he did not notice the sheep had moved away again, and it was only when the lamb was able to stand up and he wanted to give it suck, that he noticed the sheep was lying again, giving birth to another lamb. 'Oh, you devil,' gasped Little Michael, 'six pancakes.'

The second lamb was white like the first but with a black spot on its right ear. Little Michael rubbed it vigorously, pausing now and again to help the first lamb to its feet as it tried to stagger about. The sheep circled around making low noises in her throat, putting her nostrils to each lamb in turn, stopping nowhere, as giddy as a young schoolgirl, while the hard pellets of earth that stuck to her belly jingled like beads when she moved. Little Michael then took the first lamb and tried to put it to suck, but it refused to take the teat, stupidly sticking its mouth into the wool. Then he put his finger in its mouth and gradually got the teat in with his other hand. Then he pressed the teat and the hot milk squirted into the lamb's mouth. The lamb shook its tail, shrugged its body, made a little drive with its head, and began to suck.

Little Michael was just going to give the second lamb suck, when the sheep moaned and moved away again. He said 'Chowin, chowin, poor chowin,' and put the lamb to her head, but she turned away moaning and grinding her teeth and stamping. 'Oh, you devil,' said Little Michael, 'she is going to have another lamb.'

The sheep lay down again, with her foreleg stretched out in front of her and, straining her neck backwards, gave birth to a third lamb, a black lamb.

Then she rose smartly to her feet, her two sides hollow now. She shrugged herself violently and, without noticing the lambs, started to eat grass fiercely, just pausing now and again to say 'mah-m-m-m.'

Little Michael, in an ecstasy of delight, rubbed the black lamb until it was able to stand. Then he put all the lambs to suck, the sheep eating around her in a circle, without changing her feet, smelling a lamb now and again. 'Oh, you devil,' Little Michael kept saying, thinking he would be quite famous now, and talked about for a whole week. It was not every day that a sheep had three lambs.

He brought them to a sheltered spot under the fence. He wiped the birth slime from his hands with some grass. He opened his penknife and cut the dirty wool from the sheep's udder, lest the lambs might swallow some and die. Then he gave a final look at them, said, 'Chowin, chowin,' tenderly, and turned to go.

He was already at the gap when he stopped with a start. He raced back to the lambs and examined each of them. 'Three she lambs,' he gasped. 'Oh, you devil, that never happened before. Maybe father will give me half-a-crown.'

And as he raced homeward, he barked like a dog in his delight.

First Fish

AISLING MAGUIRE 1989

Fishing is taken very seriously by the men in the story. The little boy is given his first taste of the men's world. He is proud to be part of it but bewildered by what happens. His family intend the day as an initiation but they do not know what terrors it will awaken.

Someone came to wake him. It was the middle of the night and the sky was still dark except for a very small bit of sun spilt like paint across the blackness. Inside his head was dark. It wanted to close eyes and fall back to sleep. Why did they wake him? He tried to remember. Suddenly the reason was there in his head. Fishing.

'Tomorrow we will take him fishing,' one had said.

'What, the lad?' said another one.

'Why not? It's time he came.'

'Be easy on him, so.'

Now he was hurrying. He was pulling on his clothes. They puckered along his back and he started again. He was panting by the time he was finished. One came into his room again and pulled out more clothes, his winter clothes – thick jumpers and socks, even a hat with a pom-pom on the top.

They gave him porridge for breakfast. He did not like porridge. This morning he ate it without a word because everyone was eating. No one was talking. They emptied spoons of the yellowish mixture into their mouths, which opened and closed, opened and closed. He saw their pink tongues and their crooked teeth all spotted with yellow. He looked around and grinned. One of them pointed a spoon, first at him and then at his bowl. He bowed his head and went on eating.

Boots. The smell of tall green boots and short yellow boots and dainty black boots. That was a cold-weather smell. It belonged beside chestnuts and paper-dry leaves and the dark smoke of bonfires. The men put on boots and so did he. His boots were too small. He did not remember them pinching like this before.

He was lifted into the car and squeezed onto broad knees. For a moment there was darkness again as his hat was knocked down over his eyes, but he

On the West Coast

pushed it up on his forehead and looked out the window. Sunlight was beginning to grow and he saw the steams lifting up off the grasses and the cowpats. In hedges the spiders' webs trapped drops of water and flower buds were barely opened. He saw the houses standing up on top of their shadows, and he knew that where the curtains were pulled people were still sleeping.

The car stopped at the side of the lake. The fishing rods and the reels rattled loud in the air. He had never seen the lake so flat. It was smooth like skin. The islands held still like rafts jammed with a pole. When the boat pushed off, waves drew a shiver across the surface.

One dropped a bright orange life-jacket over his head. Now two of the men laughed and the other two took up the laughing and he smiled at them, pushing his hat up on his forehead. He was picked up and set down again between the big knees. He rested his elbows on the knees and opened his lips a little. The cold breeze blew inside his mouth. He shut his eyes in the first warm touch of the sun and inside himself something was lifting and bobbing, like a bubble on the water. When he opened his eyes the boat was stopped. The shore was far away. Nobody spoke. He leaned over the side till his face looked up at him from the water. It would not let him see to the bottom of the lake.

'Lakes have no bottom,' a person had told him once.

'And where do they begin?' he had asked.

'They have no beginning, only the water running down from the mountain.'

'And where do they end?' he had asked again.

'They have no beginning and they have no end. They just go on being lakes, always lakes.'

He looked now through his reflected eyes but there was nothing, only a deep, moving darkness and spots of yellow light and weed branches waving. He was pulled back. He stood sideways between the big knees. A long fishing rod was placed between his feet and his hands were made to grip the cork handle. A whirring noise started up. His hands were brought high above his head, and for one second the rod was going to fly out of his grip. He clung hard and the knees pressed his chest and his back, and with a thin water-sound something dropped and the rod sprang back. He squirmed between the knees. He wanted to look over the side and see what it was had landed in the water, but a hand drew him back and another hand tightened over his own two, keeping them stuck, till the rod felt like part of his arm.

He stood still and his legs and arms turned into stone. Nothing in the landscape changed except the streaked clouds sliding over the sky. He turned his head slowly to see the men. He did not know them any more. Their backs were bowed and their faces stayed in the one hard look. One put a hand on his head and twisted it so that he looked out across the lake again. He waited and listened and wondered. What had happened to the day? The men had made it stop. With their rods and their faces they had made everything stop. Soon he knew he would not be able to move at all, not even his head. They would make him stop too.

When they landed on the island he was happy. He pulled the life-jacket over his head and the woollen hat fell off. He pulled off his jumper and his pinching boots. His legs and feet wanted to run, to run and run in circles. His toes felt the cold of the stones and the clay. The men gave him lunch from a basket: two big sandwiches and a slice of cake. He held these in his hands and walked around. The men's voices were loud with laughter and talk, filling the air with noise. They lay out under the trees, their trouser buttons open.

He climbed across the rocks and stopped when he came to a small beach where the sand was as white as sugar. Scooping up a handful, he put it into his mouth but spat it out straightaway. The taste was of nothing and the stuff gritted in his teeth and stayed there, drying his tongue. He cupped water in his hands and lapped it to clear the sand from his mouth. He lay on his stomach and lapped again, and squinted his eye along the surface of the lake.

That was when it happened. Out of the lake a quick silver shape leaped. For one second his eye saw the fish, and his breath held as it arched and dropped down again to the lake. His skin prickled itself. Under the lake he knew someone was flinging and catching the fish.

The men were loading the boat. His boots pinched tighter now and the orange life-jacket pressed on his chest. His face felt hot.

'I want to stay here,' he said.

The men went on pushing the boat into the water.

'I want to stay here,' he said a second time.

'Well you can't stay, lad,' said the one who picked him up.

When his feet lifted off the ground he screamed. Underneath him the faces of the men blurred and disappeared and he heard their laughter. Sobs heaved through his body wanting to burst him.

Once more the boat stopped at the centre of the lake. Rods whirred and swung and the men sat bowed and made their faces hard. Small waves punched and swayed the boat. Grey clouds pressed down over the mountains and the water turned deep mud-brown. He was clamped again between strong knees and the rod was set at his feet. Then the line lifted and dragged and landed in the water. His sobbing was finished. He sniffled and tried to look at the rod. As he watched, the cork handle jumped and wagged, then stopped stiff upright. A pain trembled through his arms. His hands were wrapped tight to the rod making him hold on, making the pain bolt through to his shoulders, and the line was pulling him, pulling him up off the bottom of the boat. He screamed and large hands gripped his wrist. He twisted his head and his cheek grazed along the man's chin. The man grinned. A fierce prickling covered his skin, he shut his eyes, he was lifted and he pressed his body closer to the man's. He waited any minute now to feel the cold waves splash against his face as the line would drag him headfirst through the water that never ended.

Everything was silent now. There was a hand on his hand and a knob turning in his fingers. As he opened his eyes a silver shape rode upwards through the waves. With snaps and jerks the fish sprang up and hung before his face. His eye looked straight into a soft black eye and the eye fixed its look on him. And all the while as the man prised the mouth open and felt for the hook, the fish watched only him. That eye accused him. The man dropped the fish and the flat body thumped its own drumbeat on the floor of the boat.

It was a beautiful fish. He reached his hand down to touch the shining wet body and a cluster of glassy scales stuck to his finger. He wanted to send it back into its water. Someone pushed his hand aside and swung the fish high over his head, and the flagging tail scattered wet drops everywhere. Then the big hand slammed the fish down onto the seat. Instantly, the other hand flew up, gripping a lump of wood. That hand fell and the boat heaved with the thud of its fall.

He could not see what had happened but the drumbeat had stopped. The man turned and called to him. A sudden new stillness filled the air. Everywhere there was silence. He did not want to go to the bench but he had to see, he had to be sure he knew what the men had done.

One wide fish eye stared upwards reflecting the clouds from the sky. Small grains of sand stuck to its dark edge. He wanted to brush them off, but now his hands could not move to touch the hard, still body.

Connemara Trout by Albert Power (marble)

The Trout

SEÁN O'FAOLÁIN 1947

Childhood can be a time of intensely conflicting emotions but in this gentle tale Julia shows her growing maturity and sensitivity towards people and nature. Magic fish and magic wells are part of Irish folklore but Julia is of an age to reject fairy stories. She is fiercely protective of the fish she has discovered. Nevertheless, she will not shatter her younger brother's sense of wonder.

One of the first places Julia always ran to when they arrived in G – was The Dark Walk. It is a laurel walk, very old; almost gone wild, a lofty midnight tunnel of smooth, sinewy branches. Underfoot the tough brown leaves are never dry enough to crackle: there is always a suggestion of damp and cool trickle.

She raced right into it. For the first few yards she always had the memory of the sun behind her, then she felt the dusk closing swiftly down on her so that she screamed with pleasure and raced on to reach the light at the far end; and it was always just a little too long in coming so that she emerged gasping, clasping her hands, laughing, drinking in the sun. When she was filled with the heat and glare she would turn and consider the ordeal again.

This year she had the extra joy of showing it to her small brother, and of terrifying him as well as herself. And for him the fear lasted longer because his legs were so short and she had gone out at the far end while he was still screaming and racing.

When they had done this many times they came back to the house to tell everybody that they had done it. He boasted. She mocked. They squabbled.

'Cry babby!'

'You were afraid yourself, so there!'

'I won't take you any more.'

'You're a big pig.'

'I hate you.'

Tears were threatening so somebody said, 'Did you see the well?' She opened her eyes at that and held up her long lovely neck suspiciously and decided to be incredulous. She was twelve and at that age little girls are beginning to suspect most stories: they have already found out too many, from Santa Claus to the Stork. How could there be a well! In The Dark Walk? That she had visited year after year? Haughtily she said, 'Nonsense.'

But she went back, pretending to be going somewhere else, and she found a hole scooped in the rock at the side of the walk, choked with damp leaves, so shrouded by ferns that she only uncovered it after much searching. At the back of this little cavern there was about a quart of water. In the water she suddenly perceived a panting trout. She rushed for Stephen and dragged him to see, and they were both so excited that they were no longer afraid of the darkness as they hunched down and peered in at the fish panting in his tiny prison, his silver stomach going up and down like an engine.

Nobody knew how the trout got there. Even old Martin in the kitchen-garden laughed and refused to believe that it was there, or pretended not to believe, until she forced him to come down and see. Kneeling and pushing back his tattered old cap he peered in.

'Be cripes, you're right. How the divil in hell did that fella get there?'

She stared at him suspiciously.

'You knew?' she accused; but he said, 'The divil a know,' and reached down to lift it out. Convinced, she hauled him back. If she had found it then it was her trout.

Her mother suggested that a bird had carried the spawn. Her father thought that in the winter a small streamlet might have carried it down there as a baby, and it had been safe until the summer came and the water began to dry up. She said, 'I see,' and went back to look again and consider the matter in private. Her brother remained behind, wanting to hear the whole story of the trout, not really interested in the actual trout but much interested in the story which his mummy began to make up for him on the lines of, 'So one day Daddy Trout and Mammy Trout. . . .' When he retailed it to her she said, 'Pooh.'

It troubled her that the trout was always in the same position; he had no room to turn; all the time the silver belly went up and down; otherwise he was motionless. She wondered what he ate and in between visits to Joey Pony, and the boat and a bathe to get cool, she thought of his hunger. She brought him down bits of dough; once she brought him a worm. He ignored the food. He just went on panting. Hunched over him she thought how, all the winter, while she was at school he had been in there. All the winter, in The Dark Walk, all day, all night, floating around alone. She drew the leaf of her hat down around her ears and chin and stared. She was still thinking of it as she lay in bed.

It was late June, the longest days of the year. The sun had sat still for a week, burning up the world. Although it was after ten o'clock it was still bright and still hot. She lay on her back under a single sheet, with her long legs spread, trying to keep cool. She could see the D of the moon through the fir-tree – they slept on the ground floor. Before they went to bed her mummy had told Stephen the story of the trout again, and she, in her bed, had resolutely presented her back to them and read her book. But she had kept one ear cocked.

'And so, in the end, this naughty fish who would not stay at home got bigger and bigger and bigger, and the water got smaller and smaller. . . .'

Passionately she had whirled and cried, 'Mummy, don't make it a horrible old moral story!' Her mummy had brought in a Fairy Godmother, then, who sent lots of rain, and filled the well, and a stream poured out and the trout floated away down to the river below. Staring at the moon she knew that there are no such things as Fairy Godmothers and that the trout, down in The Dark Walk, was panting like an engine. She heard somebody unwind a fishing-reel. Would the *beasts* fish him out!

She sat up. Stephen was a hot lump of sleep, lazy thing. The Dark Walk would be full of little scraps of moon. She leaped up and looked out of the window, and somehow it was not so lightsome now that she saw the dim mountains far away and the black firs against the breathing land and heard a dog say, bark-bark. Quietly she lifted the ewer of water, and climbed out the window and scuttled along the cool but cruel gravel down to the maw of the tunnel. Her pyjamas were very short so that when she splashed water it wet her ankles. She peered into the tunnel. Something alive rustled inside there. She raced in, and up and down she raced, and flurried, and cried aloud, 'Oh, Gosh, I can't find it,' and then at last she did. Kneeling down in the damp she put her hand into the slimy hole. When the body lashed they were both mad with fright. But she gripped him and shoved him into the ewer and raced, with her teeth ground, out to the other end of the tunnel and down the steep paths to the river's edge.

All the time she could feel him lashing his tail against the side of the ewer. She was afraid he would jump right out. The gravel cut into her soles until she came to the cool ooze of the river's bank where the moon-mice on the water crept into her feet. She poured out watching until he plopped. For a second he was visible in the water. She hoped he was not dizzy. Then all she saw was the glimmer of the moon in the silent-flowing river, the dark firs, the dim mountains, and the radiant pointed face laughing down at her out of the empty sky.

She scuttled up the hill, in the window, plonked down the ewer, and flew through the air like a bird into bed. The dog said bark-bark. She heard the fishing-reel whirring. She hugged herself and giggled. Like a river of joy her holiday spread before her.

In the morning Stephen rushed to her, shouting that 'he' was gone, and asking 'where' and 'how'. Lifting her nose in the air she said superciliously, 'Fairy Godmother, I suppose?' and strolled away patting the palms of her hands.

First Confession

FRANK O'CONNOR 1953

In the Irish Republic, 95 per cent of the population belongs to the Catholic Church and 40 per cent of the people of Northern Ireland shares this same faith. Children are taken to church with their families from the time they are born. When they reach the age of seven they are considered old enough to know the difference between right and wrong and so they go to church to make a first confession of sins: a tremendous coming of age. In this story the author looks back on the innocence of his childhood with humour and understanding; he shows how anticipating an event can be terrifying, especially when a smug sister keeps interfering, but neither the narrator nor his sister could have expected what really happened when he went into the confession box and shut the door.

All the trouble began when my grandfather died and my grandmother – my father's mother – came to live with us. Relations in the one house are a strain at the best of times, but, to make matters worse, my grandmother was a real old country woman and quite unsuited to the life in town. She had a fat, wrinkled old face, and, to Mother's great indignation, went round the house in bare feet – the boots had her crippled, she said. For dinner she had a jug of porter and a pot of potatoes with – sometimes – a bit of salt fish, and she poured out the potatoes on the table and ate them slowly, with great relish, using her fingers by way of a fork.

Now, girls are supposed to be fastidious, but I was the one who suffered most from this. Nora, my sister, just sucked up to the old woman for the penny she got every Friday out of the old-age pension, a thing I could not do. I was too honest, that was my trouble; and when I was playing with Bill Connell, the sergeant-major's son, and saw my grandmother steering up the path with the jug of porter sticking out from beneath her shawl, I was mortified. I made excuses not to let him come into the house, because I could never be sure what she would be up to when we went in.

When Mother was at work and my grandmother made the dinner I wouldn't touch it. Nora once tried to make me, but I hid under the table from her and took the bread-knife with me for protection. Nora let on to be very indignant (she wasn't, of course, but she knew Mother saw through her, so she sided with Gran) and came after me. I lashed out at her with the bread-knife, and after that she left me alone. I stayed there till Mother came in from work and made my dinner, but when Father came in later Nora said in a shocked voice: 'Oh, Dadda, do you know what Jackie did at dinner-time?' Then, of course, it all came out; Father gave me a flaking; Mother interfered, and for days after that he didn't speak to me and Mother barely spoke to Nora. And all because of that old woman! God knows, I was heart-scalded.

Then, to crown my misfortunes, I had to make my first confession and communion. It was an old woman called Ryan who prepared us for these. She was about the one age with Gran; she was well-to-do, lived in a big house on Montenotte, wore a black cloak and bonnet, and came every day to school at three o'clock when we should have been going home, and talked to us of hell. She may have mentioned the other place as well, but that could only have been by accident, for hell had the first place in her heart.

She lit a candle, took out a new half-crown and offered it to the first boy who would hold one finger – only one finger! – in the flame for five minutes by the school clock. Being always very ambitious I was tempted to volunteer, but I thought it might look greedy. The she asked were we afraid of holding one finger – only one finger! – in a little candle flame for five minutes and not afraid of burning all over in roasting hot furnaces for all eternity. 'All eternity! Just think of that! A whole lifetime goes by and it's nothing, not even a drop in the ocean of your sufferings.' The woman was really interesting about hell, but my attention was all fixed on the half-crown. At the end of the lesson she put it back in her purse. It was a great disappointment; a religious woman like that, you wouldn't think she'd bother about a thing like a half-crown.

Another day she said she knew a priest who woke one night to find a fellow he didn't recognise leaning over the end of his bed. The priest was a bit frightened – naturally enough – but he asked the fellow what he wanted, and the fellow said in a deep, husky voice that he wanted to go to confession. The priest said it was an awkard time and wouldn't it do in the morning, but the fellow said that last time he went to confession, there was one sin he kept back, being ashamed to mention it, and now it was always on his mind. Then the priest knew it was a bad case, because the fellow was after making a bad confession and committing a mortal sin. He got up to dress, and just then the cock crew in the yard outside, and – lo and behold! – when the priest looked round there was no sign of the fellow, only a smell of burning timber, and when the priest looked at his bed didn't he see the print of two hands burned in it? That was because the fellow had made a bad confession. This story made a shocking impression on me.

But the worst of all was when she showed us how to examine our conscience. Did we take the name of the Lord, our God, in vain? Did we honour our father and our mother? (I asked her did this include grandmothers and she said it did.) Did we love our neighbours as ourselves? Did we covet our neighbour's goods? (I thought of the way I felt about the penny that Nora got every Friday.) I decided that, between one thing and another, I must have broken the whole ten commandments, all on account of that old woman, and so far as I could see, so long as she remained in the house I had no hope of ever doing anything else.

I was scared to death of confession. The day the whole class went I let on to have a toothache, hoping my absence wouldn't be noticed; but at three o'clock, just as I was feeling safe, along comes a chap with a message from Mrs Ryan that I was to go to confession myself on Saturday and be at the chapel for communion with the rest. To make it worse, Mother couldn't come with me and sent Nora instead.

Now, that girl had ways of tormenting me that Mother never knew of. She held my hand as we went down the hill, smiling sadly and saying how sorry she was for me, as if she were bringing me to the hospital for an operation.

'Oh, God help us!' she moaned. 'Isn't it a terrible pity you weren't a good boy? Oh, Jackie, my heart bleeds for you! How will you ever think of all your sins? Don't forget you have to tell him about the time you kicked Gran on the shin.'

'Lemme go!' I said, trying to drag myself free of her. 'I don't want to go to confession at all.'

'But sure, you'll have to go to confession, Jackie,' she replied in the same regretful tone. 'Sure, if you didn't, the parish priest would be up to the house, looking for you. 'Tisn't, God knows, that I'm not sorry for you. Do you remember the time you tried to kill me with the bread-knife under the table? And the language you used to me? I don't know what he'll do with you at all, Jackie. He might have to send you up to the bishop.'

I remember thinking bitterly that she didn't know the half of what I had to tell – if I told it. I knew I couldn't tell it, and understood perfectly why the fellow in Mrs Ryan's story made a bad confession; it seemed to me a great shame that people wouldn't stop criticising him. I remember that steep hill down to the church, and the sunlit hillsides beyond the valley of the river, which I saw in the gaps between the houses like Adam's last glimpse of Paradise.

Then, when she had manoeuvred me down the long flight of steps to the chapel yard, Nora suddenly changed her tone. She became the raging malicious devil she really was.

'There you are!' she said, with a yelp of triumph, hurling me through the church door. 'And I hope he'll give you the penitential psalms, you dirty little caffler.'

I knew then I was lost, given up to eternal justice. The door with the coloured-glass panels swung shut behind me, the sunlight went out and gave place to deep shadow, and the wind whistled outside so that the silence within seemed to crackle like ice under my feet. Nora sat in front of me by the confession box. There were a couple of old women ahead of her, and then a miserable-looking poor devil came and wedged me in at the other side, so that I couldn't escape even if I had the courage. He joined his hands and rolled his eyes in the direction of the roof, muttering aspirations in an anguished tone, and I wondered had he a grandmother too. Only a grandmother could account for a fellow behaving in that heart-broken way, but he was better off than I, for he at least could go and confess his sins; while I would make a bad confession and then die in the night and be continually coming back and burning people's furniture.

Nora's turn came, and I heard the sound of something slamming, and then her voice as if butter wouldn't melt in her mouth, and then another slam, and out she came. God, the hypocrisy of women! Her eyes were lowered, her head was bowed, and her hands were joined very low down on her stomach, and she walked up the aisle to the side altar looking like a saint. You never saw such an exhibition of devotion; and I remembered the devilish malice with which she had tormented me all the way from our door, and wondered were all religious people like that, really. It was my turn now. With the fear of damnation in my soul I went in, and the confessional door closed of itself behind me.

It was pitch-dark and I couldn't see priest or anything else. Then I really began to be frightened. In the darkness it was a matter between God and me, and He had all the odds. He knew what my intentions were before I even started; I had no chance. All I had ever been told about confession got mixed up in my mind, and I knelt to one wall and said: 'Bless me, father, for I have sinned; this is my first confession.' I waited for a few minutes, but nothing happened, so I tried it on the other wall. Nothing happened there either. He had me spotted all right.

It must have been then that I noticed the shelf at about one height with my head. It was really a place for grown-up people to rest their elbows, but in my distracted state I thought it was probably the place you were supposed to kneel. Of course, it was on the high side and not very deep, but I was always good at climbing and managed to get up all right. Staying up was the trouble. There was room only for my knees, and nothing you could get a grip on but a sort of wooden moulding a bit above it. I held on to the moulding and repeated the words a little louder, and this time something happened all right. A slide was slammed back; a little light entered the box, and a man's voice said: 'Who's there?'

''Tis me, father,' I said for fear he mightn't see me and go away again. I couldn't see him at all. The place the voice came from was under the moulding, about level with my knees, so I took a good grip of the moulding and swung myself down till I saw the astonished face of a young priest looking up at me. He had to put his head on one side to see me, and I had to put mine on one side to see him, so we were more or less talking to one another upside-down. It struck me as a queer way of hearing confessions, but I didn't feel it my place to criticise.

'Bless me, father, for I have sinned; this is my first confession,' I rattled off all in one breath, and swung myself down the least shade more to make it easier for him.

'What are you doing up there?' he shouted in an angry voice, and the strain the politeness was putting on my hold of the moulding, and the shock of being addressed in such an uncivil tone, were too much for me. I lost my grip, tumbled, and hit the door an unmerciful wallop before I found myself flat on my back in the middle of the aisle. The people who had been waiting stood up with their mouths open. The priest opened the door of the middle box and came out, pushing his biretta back from his forehead; he looked something terrible. Then Nora came scampering down the aisle.

'Oh, you dirty little caffler!' she said. 'I might have known you'd do it. I might have known you'd disgrace me. I can't leave you out of my sight for one minute.'

Before I could even get to my feet to defend myself she bent down and gave me a clip across the ear. This reminded me that I was so stunned I had forgotten to cry, so that people might think I wasn't hurt at all, when in fact I was probably maimed for life. I gave a roar out of me.

'What's all this about?' the priest hissed, getting angrier than ever and pushing Nora off me. 'How dare you hit the child like that, you little vixen?'

'But I can't do my penance with him, father,' Nora cried, cocking an outraged eye up at him.

'Well, go and do it, or I'll give you some more to do,' he said, giving me a hand up. 'Was it coming to confession you were, my poor man?' he asked me.

''Twas, father,' said I with a sob.

'Oh,' he said respectfully, 'a big hefty fellow like you must have terrible sins. Is this your first?'

''Tis, father,' said I.

'Worse and worse,' he said gloomily. 'The crimes of a lifetime. I don't know will I get rid of you at all today. You'd better wait now till I'm finished with these old ones. You can see by the looks of them they haven't much to tell.'

'I will, father,' I said with something approaching joy.

The relief of it was really enormous. Nora stuck out her tongue at me from behind his back, but I couldn't even be bothered retorting. I knew from the very moment that man opened his mouth that he was intelligent above the ordinary. When I had time to think, I saw how right I was. It only stood to reason that a fellow confessing after seven years would have more to tell than people that went every week. The crimes of a lifetime, exactly as he said. It was only what he expected, and the rest was the cackle of old women and girls with their talk of hell, the bishop, and the penitential psalms. That was all they knew. I started to make my examination of conscience, and barring the one bad business of my grandmother it didn't seem so bad.

The next time, the priest steered me into the confession box himself and left the shutter back the way I could see him get in and sit down at the further side of the grille from me.

'Well, now,' he said, 'what do they call you?'

'Jackie, father,' said I.

'And what's a-trouble to you, Jackie?'

'Father,' I said, feeling I might as well get it over with while I had him in good humour, 'I had it all arranged to kill my grandmother.'

He seemed a bit shaken by that, all right, because he said nothing for quite a while.

'My goodness,' he said at last, 'that'd be a shocking thing to do. What put that into your head?'

'Father,' I said, feeling very sorry for myself, 'she's an awful woman.'

'Is she?' he asked. 'What way is she awful?'

'She takes porter, father,' I said, knowing well from the way Mother talked of it that this was a mortal sin, and hoping it would make the priest take a more favourable view of my case.

'Oh, my!' he said, and I could see he was impressed.

'And snuff, father,' said I.

'That's a bad case, sure enough, Jackie,' he said.

'And she goes round in her bare feet, father,' I went on in a rush of self-pity, 'and she knows I don't like her, and she gives pennies to Nora and none to me, and my da sides with her and flakes me, and one night I was so heart-scalded I made up my mind I'd have to kill her.'

'And what would you do with the body?' he asked with great interest.

'I was thinking I could chop that up and carry it away in a barrow I have,' I said.

'Begor, Jackie,' he said, 'do you know you're a terrible child?'

'I know, father,' I said, for I was just thinking the same thing myself. 'I tried to kill Nora too with a bread-knife under the table, only I missed her.'

'Is that the little girl that was beating you just now?' he asked.

''Tis, father.'

'Someone will go for her with a bread-knife one day, and he won't miss her,' he said rather cryptically. 'You must have great courage. Between ourselves, there's a lot of people I'd like to do the same to but I'd never have the nerve. Hanging is an awful death.'

'Is it, father?' I asked with the deepest interest – I was always very keen on hanging. 'Did you ever see a fellow hanged?'

'Dozens of them,' he said solemnly. 'And they all died roaring.'

'Jay!' I said.

'Oh, a horrible death!' he said with great satisfaction. 'Lots of the fellows I saw killed their grandmothers too, but they all said 'twas never worth it.'

He had me there for a full ten minutes talking, and then walked out the chapel yard with me. I was genuinely sorry to part with him, because he was the most entertaining character I'd ever met in the religious line. Outside, after the shadow of the church, the sunlight was like the roaring of waves on a beach; it dazzled me; and when the frozen silence melted and I heard the screech of trams on the road my heart soared. I knew now I wouldn't die in the night and come back, leaving marks on my Mother's furniture. It would be a great worry to her, and the poor soul had enough.

Nora was sitting on the railing, waiting for me, and she put on a very sour puss when she saw the priest with me. She was mad jealous because a priest had never come out of the church with her.

'Well,' she asked coldly, after he left me, 'what did he give you?'

'Three Hail Marys,' I said.

'Three Hail Marys,' she repeated incredulously. 'You mustn't have told him anything.'

'I told him everything,' I said confidently.

'About Gran and all?'

'About Gran and all.'

(All she wanted was to be able to go home and say I'd made a bad confession.)

'Did you tell him you went for me with the bread-knife?' she asked with a frown.

'I did to be sure.'

'And he only gave you three Hail Marys?'

'That's all.'

She slowly got down from the railing with a baffled air. Clearly, this was beyond her. As we mounted the steps back to the main road she looked at me suspiciously.

'What are you sucking?' she asked.

'Bullseyes.'

'Was it the priest gave them to you?'

''Twas.'

'Lord God,' she wailed bitterly, 'some people have all the luck! 'Tis no advantage to anybody trying to be good. I might just as well be a sinner like you.'

The Half-Crown

JAMES PLUNKETT 1977

This story takes place in the centre of Dublin, around Grafton Street and St Stephen's Green. The busy city is surrounded by the beauty of sea and mountains. It is to this beauty that Michael wants to escape, to share an outing with his friends and to impress the girls. He dreams of the nearby seaside of Sandycove and Bray with its hills and cliffs. But he has just left school and is without a job. His parents have little money to give him – he needs half a crown, a coin which was worth more than a week's pocket money in those days. Michael takes out his frustration on his family and turns to desperate ways to get the money.

The man in the bookshop was suspicious. He had his hands in the pockets of his grey overall and he looked at you in a sharp knowing way which made you feel guilty.

'*A Hall and Knight's Algebra*,' Michael, embarrassed, said.

The eyes, cold and commercial, looked from the book to Michael. 'Hocking it. Slipping it out of the house to flog it for cigarettes and the pictures,' said the eyes. The hand took the book.

'A shilling,' the man said, and sucked his tooth.

'That's not enough,' Michael said, 'it's worth more than that. It's worth three bob at least.' The man turned the book over, pretending to examine it. He saw that Michael's sports jacket was too small for him and the ends of his flannel trousers were turned down in an attempt to conceal their shortness.

'Name and address?' he asked, as though absent-mindedly. That was written inside the cover. But if they really enquired and they got to know at home?

'What's that necessary for?' Michael countered. 'You don't think I stole it?'

'I'm entitled to ask that,' the man said. 'Lots of books is pinched this time of the year. Besides,' he added, 'maybe your mammy doesn't know you're selling it.' He used the word 'mammy' very deliberately as an insult to Michael's self-esteem. 'Well,' he said, 'how about one-and-sixpence?'

'It's worth more than one-and-six,' Michael persisted doggedly. The man handed it back. 'There you are,' he said without interest, 'take it or leave it.' That was that.

The previous evening he had been so certain of getting at least half a crown that he had told Anne Fox he would meet her at the station. He had been out swimming with Mark, her brother, at Sandycove and when they came back she stood on the steps to talk to them. He had leaned over the borrowed bicycle with the togs and towel wrapped about the handlebars, enticed by her dark eyes, her slim bare knees, and moved by the cool and salty odour of his own body. He would risk a lot to be with her. Getting half a crown had seemed a small enough task. He thought she was very beautiful. At one point the thought so absorbed him that she said to him smiling, 'A penny for them, Michael.' But he had no words as yet for graciousness.

It had been the first thought to come into his mind when he was wakened too early that morning by his mother's hand stirring his shoulder. She was taking the child to the dispensary and wanted to be down early to be well placed in the queue.

'Michael son,' she said at a quarter to eight. 'Michael!' But the sun even at that hour was so strong in the bedroom he found it difficult to open his eyes. Without any intention of moving he said he was coming. At half past eight she again called him. 'Your father has gone ages ago. You promised me you'd get up early,' she said. But he pulled his shoulder away to show her how he hated her to touch him. Gradually over the past year he had felt hatred of her growing in him.

'I'm coming,' he said angrily, 'go and leave me alone.' And when she had closed the door he turned over deliberately on his side. She had to be shown that shaking him would get her nowhere. But after a while, his anxiety to ask her for money had overcome his anger and he got up. She had fried bread for breakfast because it would save butter, and when he sat down at table she served him with her hat and coat on. She had the baby in the pram. The rest of the children were with her married sister in the country. He said to her:

'We're going on an outing today. I want to know if you can give me half a crown.'

'Half a crown,' she said unhappily. 'You got your pocket money on Saturday.'

'You don't call one-and-sixpence pocket money.'

That rebuffed her for a moment. She made another effort.

'Can't you borrow a bicycle somewhere?'

'We're going to Bray,' he said. 'The rest are going on the three o'clock train.'

'Couldn't you arrange to meet them out there?'

Meet them out there? Tell them he had finished with school and could find no work and he couldn't help it if it meant being short of cash? He flung fried bread across the table.

'Keep your lousy half-crown,' he said, rising to go into the bathroom.

'Michael,' she called after him, 'you know if I had it I'd give it to you.' He refused to answer. Then in a hurt tone she called to him, 'I gave you two shillings last week.' But he banged the door loudly. Later he had heard her take the pram down the steps by herself.

He stuffed the book back in his pocket. The sun, high over the tall buildings and the summer crowds, beat down on his bare head. Even under the striped awnings outside the shops in Grafton Street it was intolerably hot. There was an aroma of coffee in the air to stir his appetite, and flowers blazed yellow and red in vendors' baskets. Near the Green two girls on bicycles looked at him with interest. One was a tidy piece but she wasn't as nice as Anne Fox. He wouldn't think of Anne Fox in that way. None of the girls was as nice as Anne Fox. She was different. She wouldn't do that – no – she wouldn't let you – no. But if he couldn't go to Bray maybe Dorgan would see her home. He got on easily with girls and when he knew Michael was soft on Anne he would make sure to cut in on him. Dorgan loved to do that. He would invent stories for the rest of the gang, which he could tell in a way that made it hard not to believe them. If he did he would break his bloody neck. Then of course the rest would think it was sour grapes, but it wasn't that at all. Anne wouldn't let you do that; she was a nice girl but she was soft on him too. He knew by the way she looked at him last night on the steps, and the way she leaned her head back a little so that he could see her soft warm shapely throat and the way she laughed at what he said to show she liked him to talk to her. So nice it had been last night on the high steps under the green-gold, cloud-crossed evening sky to ask her; and now it was all being bagged-up because of a lousy half-crown.

His father and mother were both at the table. He walked through quietly to sneak the book back on the shelf. The baby was asleep in the pram. It had blobs of white ointment on its face. Bits of bun lay on its dress and coverlet. He took his place and his mother rose immediately to fetch his meal for him. The tassels of a faded green cover hung down beneath the table-cloth. There was a hole worn in the centre when the table-cloth was not on but you covered it with a fern pot and that was more or less all right. He looked at his father slyly with the idea of putting out a hint for some money but his father's face was not a good-humoured one – in fact – no – it wasn't. His father's face was moist and flabby. Though it was so warm he wore a dark suit and a butterfly collar which was respectable because of his calling. He was a clerk in the office of Joshua Bright & Son, Timber Merchants. In good humour he told stories which always ended in Mr Bright saying, 'Kavanagh: you're a man after my own heart. How on earth did you fix it? I'm certainly indebted,' or words to that effect. It always made you want to kick both of them in the fanny. But Bright was not on the menu today. There was something else.

'If I've told you once,' began his father, 'I've told you a dozen times that a razor should be dried and cleaned when you've finished with it. No one with manners a cut above those of a pig would leave a razor in the condition mine was left in. I've never objected to you using it – though what in God's name you have to shave is beyond me – all I ask is that you dry it after you.'

He remembered he had not dried it. He had left it down to put water on his hair in the absence of hair dressing and of course he forgot – well, he didn't exactly forget but he was in a bad humour over his mother.

'Razor?' he lied, pointlessly and brazenly. 'I never touched your razor.'

His father turned to his mother. 'There's your rearing for you now,' he said, 'the lie springs easy to his lips. If he's going to sit there . . . '

His mother immediately tried to conciliate them. Too quickly, in her desire to placate them, his mother said, 'You might have left it yourself, you were in such a hurry this morning.'

'That's right,' his father shouted, and let the knife and fork fall with a clatter on the plate, 'stick up for him. Encourage him to deceive and defy his own father. I'll be a bloody lunatic before long between the pair of you.'

'You can think what you like,' Michael persisted. 'It wasn't me.'

'Michael,' put in his mother.

'Then I suppose it was the cat,' his father said with childish sarcasm, 'or maybe it walked out of the case by itself. But I'll tell you one thing, you'll use it no more. You can get a razor of your own.'

'I suppose you'll tell me how.'

'Buy one. Do a little study to fit yourself for earning your keep.'

'You must have studied a bit yourself in your day,' Michael sneered. 'You earn such a hell of a lot now.'

He left the table. As he entered the next room a cup flew past his ear and shattered against the wall. It was unexpected and he jumped.

'You impertinent brat!' his father yelled after him. He locked the door hastily.

He came out when he was certain his father had gone. His mother took his meal from the oven where she had put it to keep it hot. She had been crying. That sort of thing had never happened before.

'Have your meal, child,' she said. 'I don't know what's to become of us.'

'I don't want it.'

'It isn't right to answer your father like that; you should respect him. He works hard for what he gets.'

'He knows how to hold on to it too.'

She was silent. Then she said: 'You know you'd get the half-crown if we had it. What were you ever denied that we had to give?'

'You can buy that baby in there sweet cake.'

'A little penny bun. I'm ashamed of you, Michael.'

That, unaccountably, slipped under his guard and stung him.

'You mind your own bloody business,' he lashed back.

In St Stephen's Green, children, their nurses watching them, were feeding the ducks from paper bags. And at the pond with the artificial sprays which spurted threads of pearly bright water into the thirsty air, children were sailing a boat. Michael lounged with his hands in his pockets. They were catching the train now.

'Michael Kavanagh is awful to be late like this,' the girls were saying with angry little jerks of their heads, and the fellows were saying, 'Oh, he'll come, don't bother, let's get a carriage.' They were going to Bray to swim and after to lie in the bracken. They were going to eat ice cream and drink lemonade which the boys would buy for the girls, and eat sandwiches and make tea which the girls would bring for the boys. Anne would lie in the bracken. For the length of his own afternoon he could watch the people sleeping with newspapers over their faces and look at the flowers which blazed with a barren and uncommunicative joyousness. The sculptured face of Mangan brought some lines to his mind. 'I could scale the blue air. I could walk . . . climb . . . I could . . .' How the hell did it go? That was school. You knew these things when you sat for Leaving Cert. and then after a while you wondered how the hell did it go. You left school and watched the advertisements:

Junior clerk reqd. rep. firm Hons. Leaving Cert. Knowledge book-keeping asset. 15s. weekly to start. Good prospects.

Queue with the rest; don't stammer – oh – don't stutter – think, oh, think. Cool – be cool and smile respectfully. Self-possession is nine-tenths of the law.

Your mother had pressed your suit and sat up into the small hours ironing and darning. She had already begun a Novena to Saint Anthony. (O please, Saint Anthony, send him work: O please. O sweet and good Saint Anthony, intercede for my boy.) Your father gave you advice. He told you, take off your hat and smile easily and pleasantly. Don't fidget or sit on the edge of the chair, which wasn't to say, of course, that you were to put your feet on the desk. He had had a word with Gussy Gallagher who was said to have tons of influence since he hit it lucky in the auctioneering business. He was reputed to be a brigadier-general or something in the Knights of Columbanus. Now and then your mother looked across.

'Pay attention to what your father is telling you,' she would say. When she ironed late at night like that her hair fell in straggles over her face, her breath caught her now and then, her forehead so white showed moistly in the steamy light.

As you sat waiting to be interviewed you kept saying like an idiot over and over again something silly – like:

'When Richelieu attained to office he was faced with the task of building a French navy.'

Like when you were a child you went to the shop repeating in case you might forget: A pint of milk – a tin of beans – a duck loaf – and a half-pound of margarine and say the margarine is for baking. (That was a lie, but it was only a little white lie if your mother told you to tell it.)

But in the end someone else, like Harte or Joe Andrews always got the job. Joe Andrews didn't know much about Richelieu, but he knew someone on the selection board with a bit more pull than Gussy Gallagher or Saint Anthony.

Knowledge weakened with winter, sickened with spring, withered and died in the hot July sun, giving place to new growths, to the contemplation of women, to long vacant hours, to quick greeds and slow lusts and jealous incessant neediness.

He sat down on one of the benches which were placed at secluded intervals along the quiet path. His mother was a silly bitch and his father a skinflint. His mother went out with his father to the pictures once a week and this was the night. It was the only night they went out but they could stay at home tonight because the other children were away and he was damned if he was going to stay in to mind the baby. That would be one way of getting his own back. The whole set-up was a bloody cod.

There was a thin white line running down the right side of his face, from his nose to the corner of his lips. He tried to relieve the tautness from time to time by rubbing his face with his hands, but failed because it welled up from inside him. Over him hung a wealth of almond blossom and opposite to him was a laburnum tree. It showered with perfect grace of movement to the tips of its trailing branches. Near it sat an old man and a child. He was a white-haired, serene-faced old man, whose ample waistcoat was crossed by two golden chains. On one end of the chain hung a watch. The little child was playing with it. She put it to her ear, listened, laughed. 'Tick, tock, tick, tock,' the old man said, making an attempt to imitate the sound. Frequently he bent down to chuck her under the chin or smile at her. Growing tired of the watch, she put her hand in his pocket to pull out a pair of glasses, a white handkerchief and a silver coin. The glasses and handkerchief were discarded, but she kept the coin. When she threw it, it flashed in the sun; when it fell, it rang musically on the path and rolled round and round. It staggered in circles before flopping down. The old man, whom you knew to be old more by the stringy looseness of the neck behind his white butterfly collar than by any sign of age in the bright face, smiled an invitation to Michael to enjoy the antics of the child. But Michael only hated the child. He hated the child because a foolish and indulgent old man allowed it to play carelessly with a precious piece of silver. The milled edges of a half-crown were strong and comforting. You could stand a girl's fare and buy her an ice cream, or buy cigarettes to smoke after a swim, and fish and chips to eat from a paper bag on the way home with the lads at night. The coin went up and down and he followed it greedily with his eyes. Sometimes it fell, a bright though tiny star, out of the child's reach, and the child would toddle across innocently to retrieve it. Sometimes when it fell, it staggered clumsily towards Michael. When the game had gone on for some time the old man lost interest and began to nod. Michael looked up and down the path. A keeper was examining a flower-bed some distance away. There was nobody near. But to rise, take up the coin and walk away quickly – that would be too obvious. The child might cry, or the old man open his eyes at the wrong moment. With half-closed eyes he followed the course of the coin.

To steal a half-crown could be mortal or venial. Three conditions were required for mortal sin and these were: (1) grave matter; (2) perfect knowledge; (3) full consent. It would be mortal to steal it from a poor man, but venial to steal it from a rich man, because it was dependent on the gravity of the injustice done. Not that he cared whether it was mortal or venial because he had committed sins of impurity which were always mortal and killed the soul, and it was eight months since his last confession. Automatically he almost said, 'and I accuse myself of my sins.' When the slide went click in the darkness the priest didn't say a penny for them he said well my child and with tongue stuck to roof and sweat of shame you had to tell. If you were caught you were a (not-nice-word) thief.

The coin fell and rolled towards him. He watched it. It curved, glittering, towards his left. Gingerly he reached out his foot and stopped it. Then he looked sharply at the old man, whose eyes were still closed. He bent and picked it up.

'Go on,' he whispered to the child when she came near him, 'hump off.' The face upturned to him was tiny and questioning. He could have raised his boot and crushed it without caring. But her bewilderment frightened him. When she began to cry he jumped up and said to her, 'Here – we'll look for it in the grass.'

He was earnestly searching along the verge when the old man stood beside him.

'Poor little pet,' he said, 'what's the matter now?'

'She lost her half-crown. I think it rolled in here.'

They hunted for a considerable time. Michael kept his face averted. His heart thumped. He was afraid the old man might see it there thumping against his ribs, pulsing in his neck, calling out 'thief, thief' so loudly that it must surely be heard. But the child began to sob and the old man comforted her by promising to bring her off to buy ice cream. After some time he told Michael he would have to leave it for the sweeper. 'Finders keepers,' he said regretfully but pleasantly as he was going.

Waiting impatiently while the old man and the child went off, Michael sat down again. He had no notion of the time. He should have asked the old fool before he went. They had gone in the direction of the station, but he would not dare to go that way lest they should meet again. The old man would want to chat. Where did he live? Was he still at school? What were his intentions? Suitable openings were hard to find for a young man standing on the threshold of life. A grunt. A stammer. There were no other answers to these things, none that he had found. They were simple expressions of amiability which always made the machinery of his mind lumber and clank, defeated and chaotic. He could never find responses. He was afraid if the old man spoke to him, he would blurt out: 'I took the half-crown and I'm sticking to it. You can do what you like about it.' So he sat for half an hour and then went off in the opposite direction, taking a roundabout way to the station. He passed the university where Mark would soon begin to study to be a doctor. He always had money. Mark would never need to put his foot on a half-crown dropped by a child in a public park.

The street was so quiet he could hear his own footsteps echoing, and the building itself seemed peacefully asleep. There was a smell of dust and a sunlit silence. He thought of cool waters, of Anne Fox in her red bathing costume raising her round arms to let cool water fall from them glitteringly. She would climb Bray Head in her light cotton frock, slim knees bending, a sea-fragrance about her. It would not be easy to find them. She might go anywhere about the Head to lie in the bracken. She might lie in the bracken with Dorgan. He would have to search and search.

He hastened up the steps to the station, as though by hastening he could persuade the train to leave any earlier, or be with her any sooner. But when he reached the top he stood still. Just turning away from the booking office, holding the child by the hand, was the old man. The child wanted to carry the tickets. On the steps, an impassable barrier, stood guilt and terror. Instinctively and immediately he moved away.

At the corner of the Green, leaning against one of the pillars which had held the ornamental chains that one time bordered the pavement, he remained for a long time. He knew it was after six o'clock because people were passing in clusters on bicycles, and the hunger pains in his belly were worse. He should have taken his dinner. He was staring at the sky, golden and tranquil behind barred clouds, when his mother stopped beside him. She had been shopping and was pushing the pram with the baby in it. He knew it was she but barely moved to acknowledge her. Let her see him miserable. Let her see that he had only a corner to stand at and a sky to stare into. It would hurt her and that was something to know. Once he had loved them. When he was young, before the other children came along, he and his mother had often waited for his father at that very corner with a flask of tea and sandwiches and hot currant buns. They used to go into the Green to sit on the grass and have a picnic. But now he hated them. He had nothing to say to them. He had hated them for a long time now but they refused to recognise it. His mother waited. Then she said,

'A penny for them, Michael.'

Anne Fox had said that too, and now she was lying in the bracken with Dorgan. He made a sullen mask of his face and refused to answer. After a while, this time more urgently, she said, 'Michael.'

He grunted and shrugged.

'The baby isn't well,' she began, once again placating him, trying to soften him, to bring him back to her. 'I think I'll stay in tonight. You can go to the pictures instead. Make it up with your father at tea and then the pair of you can go off together.'

'What is there to make up?' he asked. 'You make me sick.'

Hesitantly she suggested, 'You weren't very nice to him at dinner.'

'He wasn't very nice to me – was he?'

He looked around as he asked and was shocked to see tears in her eyes. But she averted her head and began to walk. He lagged behind, refusing to walk beside her. He saw in hunger and misery the squat steeple of the Methodist church, and over it the sky crossed regularly with clouds – a painted sea. Girls in the sea were slim and lovely. Girls in the sea had straight slim shapely legs. He looked at his mother's legs. They were very thin. They were encased in cheap unfashionable stockings, woolly, yellow in colour, wrinkled above the calves, much darned and dragged at the ankles. Her skirt was uneven as it swung about them. He watched the effort of her short step-by-step movement. He could not remember ever having looked at his mother's legs before. Now it stabbed him like a sword. His throat contracted. He searched for something brutal to say, something to protect himself against this fresh and unexpected onslaught of pain. She walked with her thin back towards him, her hands guiding the pram.

'We'll have to hurry home,' she said brightly; 'your poor father will be ages waiting.'

He hoped to God she had wiped her eyes. He did not want people to see her. She quickened her pace and panted with the initial push.

'I have an egg for your tea,' she added.

The brutality in him subsided. An egg for his tea. It made him want to laugh. But it also made him want to stretch out his hand to her, to touch her, to tell her he was sorry. But there were no words. He cast around for words. But when he even tried to think of them the grinding and turmoil in his head only became worse. Then his fingers touched the stolen half-crown. A flush of shame and unworthiness crept sullenly into his cheeks. It was suddenly without value. It could not buy what he wanted. Because he hardly knew what he wanted. He struggled with his own tears. He watched her now with immense tenderness, sorry for her, aching with love for her. But still something, his pride or his great shyness, would not permit him to speak to her or even to walk beside her.

In that way they went home; she walking ahead and unwitting, and he, who had no words for anything except churlishness or anger, followed silently.

The Story of the Widow's Son

MARY LAVIN 1974

Family relationships can be so intense that it is difficult to disentangle pride, jealousy, self-sacrifice, hatred and love. When her son has the chance to escape from the limitations of rural life to go to a grand school, Packy's widowed mother is a passionate confusion of such emotions, brought to a crisis as a terrible accident happens. But would it have been any different if another accident had happened instead . . . ?

This is the story of a widow's son, but it is a story that has two endings.

There was once a widow, living in a small neglected village at the foot of a steep hill. She had only one son, but he was the meaning of her life. She lived for his sake. She wore herself out working for him. Every day she made a hundred sacrifices in order to keep him at a good school in the town, four miles away, because there was a better teacher there than the village dullard that had taught herself.

She made great plans for Packy, but she did not tell him about her plans. Instead she threatened him, day and night, that if he didn't turn out well, she would put him to work on the roads, or in the quarry under the hill.

But as the years went by, everyone in the village, and even Packy himself, could tell by the way she watched him out of sight in the morning, and watched to see him come into sight in the evening, that he was the beat of her heart, and that her gruff words were only a cover for her pride and her joy in him.

It was for Packy's sake that she walked for hours along the road, letting her cow graze the long acre of the wayside grass, in order to spare the few poor blades that pushed up through the stones in her own field. It was for his sake she walked back and forth to the town to sell a few cabbages as soon as ever they were fit. It was for his sake that she got up in the cold dawning hours to gather mushrooms that would take the place of foods that had to be bought with money. She bent her back daily to make every penny she could, and as often happens, she made more by industry, out of her few bald acres, than many of the farmers around her made out of their great bearded meadows. Out of the money she made by selling eggs alone, she paid for Packy's clothes and for the great number of his books.

Bus Stop by Martin Gale

When Packy was fourteen, he was in the last class in the school, and the master had great hopes of his winning a scholarship to a big college in the city. He was getting to be a tall lad, and his features were beginning to take a strong cast. His character was strengthening too, under his mother's sharp tongue. The people of the village were beginning to give him the same respect they gave to the sons of the farmers who came from their fine colleges in the summer, with blue suits and bright ties. And whenever they spoke to the widow they praised him up to the skies.

One day in June, when the air was so heavy the scent that rose up from the grass was imprisoned under the low clouds and hung in the air, the widow was waiting at the gate for Packy. There had been no rain for some days and the hens and chickens were pecking irritably at the dry ground and wandering up and down the road in bewilderment.

A neighbour passed.

'Waiting for Packy?' said the neighbour, pleasantly, and he stood for a minute to take off his hat and wipe the sweat of the day from his face. He was an old man.

'It's a hot day!' he said. 'It will be a hard push for Packy on that battered old bike of his. I wouldn't like to have to face into four miles on a day like this!'

'Packy would travel three times that distance if there was a book at the other end of the road!' said the widow, with the pride of those who cannot read more than a line or two without wearying.

The minutes went by slowly. The widow kept looking up at the sun.

'I suppose the heat is better than the rain!' she said, at last.

'The heat can do a lot of harm, too, though,' said the neighbour, absent-mindedly, as he pulled a long blade of grass from between the stones of the wall and began to chew the end of it.

'You could get sunstroke on a day like this!' He looked up at the sun. 'The sun is a terror,' he said. 'It could cause you to drop down dead like a stone!'

The widow strained out further over the gate. She looked up the hill in the direction of the town.

'He will have a good cool breeze on his face coming down the hill, at any rate,' she said.

The man looked up the hill. 'That's true. On the hottest day of the year you would get a cool breeze coming down that hill on a bicycle. You would feel the air streaming past your cheeks like silk. And in the winter it's like two knives flashing to either side of you, and peeling off your skin like you'd peel the bark off a sally-rod.' He chewed the grass meditatively. 'That must be one of the steepest hills in Ireland,' he said. 'That hill is a hill worthy of the name of a hill.' He took the grass out of his mouth. 'It's my belief,' he said, earnestly, looking at the widow – 'it's my belief that that hill is to be found marked with a name in the Ordnance Survey map!'

'If that's the case,' said the widow, 'Packy will be able to tell you all about it. When it isn't a book he has in his hand it's a map.'

'Is that so?' said the man. 'That's interesting. A map is a great thing. A map is not an ordinary thing. It isn't everyone can make out a map.'

The widow wasn't listening.

'I think I see Packy!' she said, and she opened the wooden gate and stepped out into the roadway.

At the top of the hill there was a glitter of spokes as a bicycle came into sight. Then there was a flash of blue jersey as Packy came flying downward, gripping the handlebars of the bike, with his bright hair blown back from his forehead. The hill was so steep, and he came down so fast, that it seemed to the man and woman at the bottom of the hill that he was not moving at all, but that it was the bright trees and bushes, the bright ditches and wayside grasses that were streaming away to either side of him.

The hens and chickens clucked and squawked and ran along the road looking for a safe place in the ditches. They ran to either side with feminine fuss and chatter. Packy waved to his mother. He came nearer and nearer. They could see the freckles on his face.

'Shoo!' cried Packy, at the squawking hens that had not yet left the roadway. They ran with their long necks straining forward.

'Shoo' said Packy's mother, lifting her apron and flapping it in the air to frighten them out of his way.

It was only afterwards, when the harm was done, that the widow began to think that it might, perhaps, have been the flapping of her own apron that frightened the old clucking hen, and sent her flying out over the garden wall into the middle of the road.

The old hen appeared suddenly on top of the grassy ditch and looked with a distraught eye at the hens and chickens as they ran to right and left. Her own feathers began to stand out from her. She craned her neck forward and gave a distracted squawk, and fluttered down into the middle of the hot dusty road.

Packy jammed on the brakes. The widow screamed. There was a flurry of white feathers and a spurt of blood. The bicycle swerved and fell. Packy was thrown over the handlebars.

It was such a simple accident that, although the widow screamed, and although the old man looked around to see if there was help near, neither of them thought that Packy was very badly hurt, but when they ran over and lifted his head, and saw that he could not speak, they wiped the blood from his face and looked around, desperately, to measure the distance they would have to carry him.

It was only a few yards to the door of the cottage, but Packy was dead before they got him across the threshold.

'He's only in a weakness!' screamed the widow, and she urged the crowd that had gathered outside the door to do something for him. 'Get a doctor!' she cried, pushing a young labourer towards the door. 'Hurry! Hurry! The doctor will bring him around.'

But the neighbours that kept coming in the door, quickly, from all sides, were crossing themselves, one after another, and falling on their knees, as soon as they laid eyes on the boy, stretched out flat on the bed, with the dust and dirt and the sweat marks of life on his dead face.

When at last the widow was convinced that her son was dead, the other women had to hold her down. She waved her arms and cried out aloud, and wrestled to get free. She wanted to wring the neck of every hen in the yard.

'I'll kill every one of them. What good are they to me, now? All the hens in the world aren't worth one drop of human blood. That old clucking hen wasn't worth more than six shillings, at the very most. What is six shillings? Is it worth poor Packy's life?'

But after a time she stopped raving, and looked from one face to another.

'Why didn't he ride over the old hen?' she asked. 'Why did he try to save an old hen that wasn't worth more than six shillings? Didn't he know he was worth more to his mother than an old hen that would be going into the pot one of these days? Why did he do it? Why did he put on the brakes going down one of the worst hills in the country? Why? Why?'

The neighbours patted her arm.

'There now!' they said. 'There now!' and that was all they could think of saying, and they said it over and over again.

'There now! There now!'

And years afterwards, whenever the widow spoke of her son Packy to the neighbours who dropped in to keep her company for an hour or two, she always had the same question to ask; the same tireless question.

'Why did he put the price of an old clucking hen above the price of his own life?'

And the people always gave the same answer.

'There now!' they said. 'There now!' And they sat as silently as the widow herself, looking into the fire.

But surely some of those neighbours must have been stirred to wonder what would have happened had Packy not yielded to his impulse of fear, and had, instead, ridden boldly over the old clucking hen? And surely some of them must have stared into the flames and pictured the scene of the accident again, altering a detail here and there as they did so, and giving the story a different end. For these people knew the widow, and they knew Packy, and when you know people well it is as easy to guess what they would say and do in certain circumstances as it is to remember what they actually did say and do in other circumstances. In fact it is sometimes easier to invent than to remember accurately, and were this not so two great branches of creative art would wither in an hour: the art of the story-teller and the art of the gossip. So, perhaps, if I try to tell you what I myself think might have happened had Packy killed that cackling old hen, you will not accuse me of abusing my privileges as a writer. After all, what I am about to tell you is no more of a fiction than what I have already told, and I lean no heavier now upon your credulity than, with your full consent, I did in the first instance.

And moreover, in many respects the new story is the same as the old.

It begins in the same way, too. There is the widow grazing her cow by the wayside, and walking the long roads to the town, weighed down with sacks of cabbages that will pay for Packy's schooling. There she is, fussing over Packy in the mornings in case he would be late for school. There she is in the evening watching the battered clock on the dresser for the hour when he will appear on the top of the hill at his return. And there too, on a hot day in June, is the old labouring man coming up the road, and pausing to talk to her, as she stood at the door. There he is dragging a blade of grass from between the stones of the wall, and putting it between his teeth to chew, before he opens his mouth.

And when he opens his mouth at last it is to utter the same remark.

'Waiting for Packy?' said the old man, and then he took off his hat and wiped the sweat from his forehead. It will be remembered that he was an old man. 'It's a hot day,' he said.

'It's very hot,' said the widow, looking anxiously up the hill. 'It's a hot day
to push a bicycle four miles along a bad road with the dust rising to choke
you, and the sun striking spikes off the handlebars.'

'The heat is better than the rain, all the same,' said the old man.

'I suppose it is,' said the widow. 'All the same, there were the days when
Packy came home with the rain dried into his clothes so bad they stood up stiff
like boards when he took them off. They stood up stiff like boards against the
wall, for all the world as if he was still standing in them!'

'Is that so?' said the old man. 'You may be sure he got a good petting on
those days. There is no son like a widow's son. A ewe lamb!'

'Is it Packy?' said the widow, in disgust. 'Packy never got a day's petting
since the day he was born. I made up my mind from the first that I'd never
make a soft one out of him.'

The widow looked up the hill again, and set herself to raking the gravel
outside the gate as if she were in the road for no other purpose. Then she gave
another look up the hill.

'Here he is now!' she said, and she raised such a cloud of dust with the rake
that they could hardly see the glitter of the bicycle spokes, and the flash of
blue jersey as Packy came down the hill at breakneck speed.

Nearer and nearer he came, faster and faster, waving his hand to the
widow, shouting at the hens to leave the way!

The hens ran for the ditches, stretching their necks in gawky terror. And
then, as the last hen squawked into the ditch, the way was clear for a moment
before the whirling of silver spokes.

Then, unexpectedly, up from nowhere it seemed, came an old clucking hen
and, clucking despairingly, it stood for a moment on the top of the wall and
then rose into the air with the clumsy flight of a ground fowl.

Packy stopped whistling. The widow screamed. Packy yelled and the
widow flapped her apron. Then Packy swerved the bicycle, and a cloud of
dust rose from the braked wheel.

For a minute it could not be seen what exactly had happened, but Packy put
his foot down and dragged it along the ground in the dust till he brought the
bicycle to a sharp stop. He threw the bicycle down with a clatter on the hard
road and ran back. The widow could not bear to look. She threw her apron
over her head.

'He's killed the clucking hen!' she said. 'He's killed her! He's killed her!'
and then she let the apron fall back into place, and began to run up the hill

herself. The old man spat out the blade of grass that he had been chewing and ran after the woman.

'Did you kill it?' screamed the widow, and as she got near enough to see the blood and feathers she raised her arm over her head, and her fist was clenched till the knuckles shone white. Packy cowered down over the carcass of the fowl and hunched up his shoulders as if to shield himself from a blow. His legs were spattered with blood, and the brown and white feathers of the dead hen were stuck to his hands, and stuck to his clothes, and they were strewn all over the road. Some of the short white inner feathers were still swirling with the dust in the air.

'I couldn't help it, Mother. I couldn't help it. I didn't see her till it was too late!'

The widow caught up the hen and examined it all over, holding it by the bone of the breast, and letting the long neck dangle. Then, catching it by the leg, she raised it suddenly above her head, and brought down the bleeding body on the boy's back, in blow after blow, spattering the blood all over his face and his hands, over his clothes and over the white dust of the road around him.

'How dare you lie to me!' she screamed, gaspingly, between the blows. 'You saw the hen. I know you saw it. You stopped whistling! You called out! We were watching you. We saw.' She turned upon the old man. 'Isn't that right?' she demanded. 'He saw the hen, didn't he? He saw it?'

'It looked that way,' said the old man, uncertainly, his eye on the dangling fowl in the widow's hand.

'There you are!' said the widow. She threw the hen down on the road. 'You saw the hen in front of you on the road, as plain as you see it now,' she accused, 'but you wouldn't stop to save it because you were in too big a hurry home to fill your belly! Isn't that so?'

'No, Mother. No! I saw her all right but it was too late to do anything.'

'He admits now that he saw it,' said the widow, turning and nodding triumphantly at the onlookers who had gathered at the sound of the shouting.

'I never denied seeing it!' said the boy, appealing to the onlookers as to his judges.

'He doesn't deny it!' screamed the widow. 'He stands there as brazen as you like, and admits for all the world to hear that he saw the hen as plain as the nose on his face, and he rode over it without a thought!'

'But what else could I do?' said the boy, throwing out his hand; appealing to the crowd now, and now appealing to the widow. 'If I'd put on the brakes going down the hill at such a speed I would have been put over the handlebars!'

'And what harm would that have done you?' screamed the widow. 'I often saw you taking a toss when you were wrestling with Jimmy Mack and I heard no complaints afterwards, although your elbows and knees would be running blood, and your face scraped like a gridiron!' She turned to the crowd. 'That's as true as God. I often saw him come in with his nose spouting blood like a pump, and one eye closed as tight as the eye of a corpse. My hand was often stiff for a week from sopping out wet cloths to put poultices on him and try to bring his face back to rights again.' She swung back to Packy again. 'You're not afraid of a fall when you go climbing trees, are you? You're not afraid to go up on the roof after a cat, are you? Oh, there's more in this than you want me to know. I can see that. You killed that hen on purpose – that's what I believe! You're tired of going to school. You want to get out of going away to college. That's it! You think if you kill the few poor hens we have there will be no money in the box when the time comes to pay for books and classes. That's it!' Packy began to redden.

'It's late in the day for me to be thinking of things like that,' he said. 'It's long ago I should have started those tricks if that was the way I felt. But it's not true. I want to go to college. The reason I was coming down the hill so fast was to tell you that I got the scholarship. The teacher told me as I was leaving the schoolhouse. That's why I was pedalling so hard. That's why I was whistling. That's why I was waving my hand. Didn't you see me waving my hand from once I came in sight at the top of the hill?'

The widow's hands fell to her sides. The wind of words died down within her and left her flat and limp. She didn't know what to say. She could feel the neighbours staring at her. She wished that they were gone away about their business. She wanted to throw out her arms to the boy, to drag him against her heart and hug him like a small child. But she thought of how the crowd would look at each other and nod and snigger. A ewe lamb! She didn't want to satisfy them. If she gave into her feelings now they would know how much she had been counting on his getting the scholarship. She wouldn't please them! She wouldn't satisfy them!

She looked at Packy, and when she saw him standing there before her, spattered with the furious feathers and crude blood of the dead hen, she felt a fierce disappointment for the boy's own disappointment, and a fierce resentment against him for killing the hen on this day of all days, and spoiling the great news of his success.

Her mind was in confusion. She stared at the blood on his face, and all at once it seemed as if the blood was a bad omen of the future that was for him. Disappointment, fear, resentment, and above all defiance, raised themselves within her like screeching animals. She looked from Packy to the onlookers.

'Scholarship! Scholarship!' she sneered, putting as much derision as she could into her voice and expression.

'I suppose you think you are a great fellow now? I suppose you think you are independent now? I suppose you think you can go off with yourself now, and look down on your poor slave of a mother who scraped and sweated for you with her cabbages and her hens? I suppose you think to yourself that it doesn't matter now whether the hens are alive or dead? Is that the way? Well, let me tell you this! You're not as independent as you think. The scholarship may pay for your books and your teacher's fees but who will pay for your clothes? Ah-ha, you forgot that, didn't you?' She put her hands on her hips. Packy hung his head. He no longer appealed to the gawking neighbours. They might have been able to save him from blows but he knew enough about life to know that no one could save him from shame.

The widow's heart burned at the sight of his shamed face, as her heart burned with grief, but her temper too burned fiercer and fiercer, and she came to a point at which nothing could quell the blaze till it had burned itself out. 'Who'll buy your suits?' she yelled. 'Who'll buy your boots?' She paused to think of more humiliating accusations. 'Who'll buy your breeches?' She paused again and her teeth bit against each other. What would wound deepest? What shame could she drag upon him? 'Who'll buy your nightshirts or will you sleep in your skin?'

The neighbours laughed at that, and the tension was broken. The widow herself laughed. She held her sides and laughed, and as she laughed everything seemed to take on a newer and simpler significance. Things were not as bad as they seemed a moment before. She wanted Packy to laugh too. She looked at him. But as she looked at Packy her heart turned cold with a strange new fear.

'Get into the house!' she said, giving him a push ahead of her. She wanted him safe under her own roof. She wanted to get him away from the gaping neighbours. She hated them, man, woman and child. She felt that if they had not been there things would have been different. And she wanted to get away from the sight of the blood on the road. She wanted to mash a few potatoes and make a bit of potato cake for Packy. That would comfort him. He loved that.

Packy hardly touched the food. And even after he had washed and scrubbed himself there were stains of blood turning up in the most unexpected places: behind his ears, under his finger-nails, inside the cuff of his sleeve.

'Put on your good clothes,' said the widow, making a great effort to be gentle, but her manners had become as twisted and as hard as the branches of the trees across the road from her, and even the kindly offers she made sounded harsh. The boy sat on the chair in a slumped position that kept her nerves on edge and set up a further conflict of irritation and love in her heart. She hated to see him slumping there in the chair, not asking to go outside the door, but still she was uneasy whenever he as much as looked in the direction of the door. She felt safe while he was under the roof; inside the lintel; under her eyes.

Next day she went in to wake him for school, but his room was empty; his bed had not been slept in, and when she ran out into the yard and called him everywhere there was no answer. She ran up and down. She called at the houses of the neighbours but he was not in any house. And she thought she could hear sniggering behind her in each house that she left, as she ran to another one. He wasn't in the village. He wasn't in the town. The master of the school said that she should let the police have a description of him. He said he never met a boy as sensitive as Packy. A boy like that took strange notions into his head from time to time.

The police did their best but there was no news of Packy that night. A few days later there was a letter saying that he was well. He asked his mother to notify the master that he would not be coming back, so that some other boy could claim the scholarship. He said that he would send the price of the hen as soon as he made some money.

Another letter in a few weeks said that he had got a job on a trawler, and that he would not be able to write very often but that he would put aside some of his pay every week and send it to his mother whenever he got into port. He said that he wanted to pay her back for all she had done for him. He gave no address. He kept his promise about the money but he never gave any address when he wrote.

. . . And so the people may have let their thoughts run on, as they sat by the fire with the widow, many a night, listening to her complaining voice saying the same thing over and over. 'Why did he put the price of an old hen above the price of his own life?' And it is possible that their version of the story has a certain element of truth about it, too. Perhaps all our actions have this double quality about them, this possibility of alternative, and that it is only by careful watching and absolute sincerity that we follow the path that is destined for us, and, no matter how tragic that may be, it is better than the tragedy we bring upon ourselves.

The Rug

EDNA O'BRIEN 1968

The girl in this story is very sensitive to her mother's hopes and disappointments. She does not judge her ineffectual father but relates to her mother's delight in the unexpected parcel. This provides joy and speculation to the whole household . . . for a short time.

I went down on my knees upon the brand-new linoleum, and smelled the strange smell. It was rich and oily. It first entered and attached itself to something in my memory when I was nine years old. I've since learned that it is the smell of linseed oil, but coming on it unexpectedly can make me both a little disturbed and sad.

I grew up in the west of Ireland, in a grey cut-stone farmhouse, which my father inherited from his father. My father came from lowland, better-off farming people, my mother from the wind-swept hungry hills above a great lake. As children, we played in a small forest of rhododendrons – thickened and tangled and broken under scratching cows – around the house and down the drive. The avenue up from the front gates had such great pot-holes that cars had to lurch off into the field and out again.

But though all outside was neglect, overgrown with ragwort and thistle, strangers were surprised when they entered the house; my father might fritter his life away watching the slates slip from the outhouse roofs – but, within, that safe, square, lowland house of stone was my mother's pride and joy. It was always spotless. It was stuffed with things – furniture, china dogs, toby mugs, tall jugs, trays, tapestries and whatnots. Each of the four bedrooms had holy pictures on the walls and a gold overmantel surmounting each fireplace. In the fireplaces there were paper fans or lids of chocolate boxes. Mantelpieces carried their own close-packed array of wax flowers, holy statues, broken alarm clocks, shells, photographs, soft rounded cushions for sticking pins in.

My father was generous, foolish and so idle that it could only have been some sort of illness. That year in which I was nine and first experienced the wonderful smell, he sold another of the meadows to pay off some debt, and for the first time in many years my mother got a lump of money.

She went out early one morning and caught the bus to the city, and through a summer morning and afternoon she trudged around looking at linoleums. When she came home in the evening, her feet hurting from high heels, she said she had bought some beautiful light-brown linoleum, with orange squares on it.

The day came when the four rolls were delivered to the front gates, and Hickey, our farm help, got the horse and cart ready to bring it up. We all went; we were that excited. The calves followed the cart, thinking that maybe they were to be fed down by the roadside. At times they galloped away but came back again, each calf nudging the other out of the way. It was a warm, still day, the sounds of cars and neighbours' dogs carried very distinctly and the cow-pats on the drive were brown and dry like flake tobacco.

My mother did most of the heaving and shoving to get the rolls on to the cart. She had early accepted that she had been born to do the work.

She may have bribed Hickey with the promise of hens to sell for himself, because that evening he stayed in to help with the floor – he usually went over to the village and drank a pint or two of stout. Mama, of course, always saved newspapers, and she said that the more we laid down under the lino the longer it would wear. On her hands and knees, she looked up once – flushed, delighted, tired – and said, 'Mark my words, we'll see a carpet in here yet.'

There was calculation and argument before cutting the difficult bits around the door frames, the bay window and the fireplace. Hickey said that without him my mother would have botched the whole thing. In the quick flow of argument and talk, they did not notice that it was past my bedtime. My father sat outside in the kitchen by the stove all evening while we worked. Later, he came in and said what a grand job we were doing. A grand job, he said. He'd had a headache.

The next day must have been Saturday, for I sat in the sitting-room all morning admiring the linoleum, smelling its smell, counting the orange squares. I was supposed to be dusting. Now and then I rearranged the blinds, as the sun moved. We had to keep the sun from fading the bright colours.

The dogs barked and the postman cycled up. I ran out and met him carrying a huge parcel. Mama was away up in the yard with the hens. When the postman had gone, I went up to tell her.

'A parcel?' she said. She was cleaning the hens' trough before putting their food in it. The hens were moiling around, falling in and out of the buckets, pecking at her hands. 'It's just binding twine for the baling machine,' she said. 'Who'd be sending parcels?' She was never one to lose her head.

I said that the parcel had a Dublin postmark – the postman told me that – and that there was some black woolly thing in it. The paper was torn at the corner, and I'd pushed a finger in, fearfully.

Coming down to the house she wiped her hands with a wad of long grass. 'Perhaps somebody in America has remembered us at last.' One of her few dreams was to be remembered by relatives who had gone to America. The farm buildings were some way from the house; we ran the last bit. But, even in her excitement, her careful nature forced her to unknot every length of string from the parcel and roll it up, for future use. She was the world's most generous woman, but was thrifty about saving twine and paper, and candle stumps, and turkey wings and empty pill boxes.

'My God,' she said reverently, folding back the last piece of paper and revealing a black sheepskin hearth-rug. We opened it out. It was a half-moon shape and covered the kitchen table. She could not speak. It was real sheepskin, thick and soft and luxurious. She examined the lining, studied the maker's label in the back, searched through the folds of brown paper for a possible letter, but there was nothing at all to indicate where it had come from.

'Get me my glasses,' she said. We read the address again, and the postmark. The parcel had been sent from Dublin two days before. 'Call your father,' she said. He was in bed with rheumatic pains. Rug or no rug, he demanded a fourth cup of tea before he could get up.

We carried the big black rug into the sitting-room and laid it down upon the new linoleum, before the fireplace.

'Isn't it perfect, a perfect colour scheme?' she said. The room had suddenly become cosy. She stood back and looked at it with surprise, and a touch of suspicion. Though she was always hoping, she never really expected things to turn out well. At nine years old, I knew enough about my mother's life to say a prayer of thanks that at last she had got something she wanted, and without having to work for it. She had a round, sallow face and a peculiarly uncertain, timid smile. The suspicion soon left her and the smile came out. That was one of her happiest days; I remember it as I remember her unhappiest day to my knowledge – the day the bailiff came, a year later. I hoped she would sit in the newly appointed room on Sundays for tea, without her apron, with her brown hair combed out, looking calm and beautiful. Outside, the rhododendrons, though wild and broken, would bloom red and purple and, inside, the new rug would lie upon the richly smelling linoleum. She hugged me suddenly, as if I were the one to thank for it all; the hen mash had dried on her hands and they had the mealy smell I knew so well.

For spells during the next few days, my mother racked her brain, and she racked our brains, for a clue. It had to be someone who knew something of her needs and wants – how else could he have decided upon just the thing she needed? She wrote letters here and there, to distant relations, to friends, to people she had not seen for years.

'Must be one of *your* friends,' she would say to my father.

'Oh, probably, probably. I've known a lot of decent people in my time.'

She was referring – ironically, of course – to the many strangers to whom he had offered tea. He liked nothing better than to stand down at the gates on a fair day or a race day, engaging passers-by in conversation and finally bringing someone up to the house for tea and boiled eggs. He had a genius for making friends.

'I'd say that's it,' my father said, delighted to take credit for the rug.

In the warm evenings we sat around the fireplace – we'd never had a fire in that room throughout the whole of my childhood – and around the rug, listening to the radio. And now and then, Mama or Dada would remember someone else from whom the rug might have come. Before a week had passed, she had written to a dozen people – an acquaintance who had moved up to Dublin with a greyhound pup Dada had given him, which greyhound had turned out a winner; an unfrocked priest who had stayed in our house for a week, gathering strength from Mama to travel on home and meet his family; a magician who had stolen Dada's gold watch and never been seen since; a farmer who once sold us a tubercular cow and would not take it back.

Weeks passed. The rug was taken out on Saturdays and shaken well, the new lino polished. Once, coming home early from school, I looked in the window and saw Mama kneeling on the rug saying a prayer. I'd never seen her pray like that, in the middle of the day, before. My father was going into the next county the following day to look at a horse he thought he might get cheap; she was, of course, praying that he would keep his promise and not touch a drink. If he did, he might be off on a wild progress and would not be seen for a week.

He went the next day; he was to stay overnight with relations. While he was away, I slept with Mama, for company, in the big brass bed. I wakened to see a candle flame, and Mama hurriedly putting on her cardigan. Dada had come home? No, she said, but she had been lying awake thinking, and there was something she had to tell Hickey or she would not get a wink of sleep. It was not yet twelve; he might be awake. I didn't want to be left in the dark, I said, but she was already hurrying along the landing. I nipped out of bed, and followed. The luminous clock said a quarter to twelve. From the first landing, I looked over and saw her turning the knob of Hickey's door.

Why should he open his door to her then? I thought; he never let anyone in at any time, keeping the door locked when he was out on the farm. Once we climbed in through the window and found things in such a muddle – his good suit laid out flat on the floor, a shirt soaking in a bucket of dirty green water, a milk can in which there was curdled buttermilk, a bicycle chain, a broken Sacred Heart and several pairs of worn, distorted, cast-off boots – that she resolved never to set foot in it again.

'What the hell is it?' Hickey said. Then there was a thud. He must have knocked something over while he searched for his flashlamp.

'If it's fine tomorrow, we'll cut the turf,' Mama said.

Hickey asked if she'd wakened him at that hour to tell him something he already knew – they discussed it at tea-time.

'Open the door,' she said. 'I have a bit of news for you, about the rug.'

He opened the door just a fraction. 'Who sent it?' he asked.

'That party from Ballinsloe,' she said.

'That party' was her phrase for her two visitors who had come to our house years before – a young girl, and an older man who wore brown gauntlet gloves. Almost as soon as they'd arrived, my father went out with them in their motor car. When they returned to our house an hour later, I gathered from the conversation that they had been to see our local doctor, a friend of Dada's. The girl was the sister of a nun, who was the headmistress at the convent where my sisters were. She had been crying. I guessed then, or maybe later, that her tears had to do with her having a baby and that Dada had taken her to the doctor so that she could find out for certain if she were pregnant and make preparations to get married. It would have been impossible for her to go to a doctor in her own neighbourhood, and I had no doubt but that Dada was glad to do a favour for the nun, as he could not always pay the fees for my sisters' education. Mama gave them tea on a tray – not a spread with hand-embroidered cloth and bone-china cups – and shook hands with them coolly when they were leaving. She could not abide sinful people.

'Nice of them to remember,' Hickey said, sucking air between his teeth and making bird noises. 'How did you find out?'

'I just guessed,' Mama told him.

'Oh, Christ!' Hickey said, closing his door with a fearful bang and getting back into bed with such vehemence that I could hear the springs revolt.

Mama carried me up the stairs, because my feet were cold, and said that Hickey had not one ounce of manners.

Next day, when Dada came home sober, she told him the story, and that night she wrote to the nun. In due course, a letter came to us – with holy medals and scapulars enclosed for me – saying that neither the nun nor her married sister had sent a gift. I expect the girl had married the man with the gauntlet gloves.

''Twill be one of life's mysteries,' Mama said, as she beat the rug against the pier, closed her eyes to escape the dust and reconciled herself to never knowing.

But a knock came on our back door four weeks later, when we were upstairs changing the sheets on the beds. 'Run down and see who it is,' she said.

It was a namesake of Dada's from the village, a man who always came to borrow something – a donkey, or a mowing machine, or even a spade.

'Is your mother in?' he asked, and I went half-way up the stairs and called her down.

'I've come for the rug,' he said.

'What rug?' Mama asked. It was the nearest she ever got to lying. Her breath caught short and she blushed a little.

'I hear you have a new rug here. Well, 'tis our rug, because my wife's sister sent it to us months ago and we never got it.'

'What are you talking about?' she said in a very sarcastic voice. He was a cowardly man, and it was said that he was so ineffectual he would call his wife in from the garden to pour him a cup of tea. I suppose my mother hoped that she would frighten him off.

'The rug the postman brought here one morning, and handed it to your youngster there.' He nodded at me.

'Oh, that,' Mama said, a little stunned by the news that the postman had given information about it. Then a ray of hope, a ray of lunacy, must have struck her, because she asked what colour of rug he was inquiring about.

'A black sheepskin,' he said.

There could be no more doubt about it. Her whole being drooped – shoulders, stomach, voice, everything.

'It's here,' she said absently, and she went through the hall into the sitting-room.

'Being namesakes and that, the postman got us mixed up,' he said stupidly to me.

She had winked at me to stay there and see he did not follow her, because she did not want him to know that we had been using it.

It was rolled and had a piece of cord around the middle when she handed it to him. As she watched him go down the avenue she wept, not so much for the loss – though the loss was enormous – as for her own foolishness in thinking that someone had wanted to do her a kindness at last.

'We live and learn,' she said, as she undid her apron strings, out of habit, and then retied them slowly and methodically, making a tighter knot.

Offaly Woman and Child, taken at Oughter by Fr. F.M. Browne SJ, 1929

Mr Sing My Heart's Delight

BRIAN FRIEL 1962

The old woman has lived most of her life in the midst of the bogland above the Atlantic Ocean. She shares her pleasure in nature with her young grandson and he shares his knowledge of the 'outside world' with her. Her romantic nature makes the people and events outside her world into the stuff of fairy-tale. When the travelling salesman comes to her door she is enchanted by his goods and by what she imagines of his background. Finally we see two figures whose dignity stands out clearly against their shared experience of poverty.

On the first day of every new year, I made the forty-five-mile journey by train, mail car, and foot across County Donegal to my granny's house which sat at the top of a cliff above the raging Atlantic at the very end of the parish of Mullaghduff. This annual visit, lasting from January until the nights began to shorten sometime in March, was made primarily for Granny's benefit: during those months Grandfather went across to Scotland to earn enough money to tide them over the rest of the year. But it suited me admirably too: I missed school for three months, I got away from strict parents and bothersome brothers and sisters, all younger than I, and in Granny's house I was cock-of-the-walk and eveything I did was right.

The house consisted of one room in which Granny and Grandfather lived and slept. It was a large room lit by a small window and a door which could be left open for the greater part of the day because it faced east and the winds usually blew from the west. There were three chairs, a table, a bed in the corner, a dresser, and an open hearth-fire over which stretched the mantelpiece, the focal point of the room. In such bare surroundings, that mantelpiece held a rich array. A china dog stood guard at each end and between them there was a shining silver alarm clock, two vases, a brass elf holding a cracked thermometer whose mercury had long since been spilled, a golden picture frame enclosing a coloured photograph of a racehorse, and the shells of three sea urchins, sitting on three matchboxes covered with red crêpe paper. Every year I went there, I had to have each of those pieces handed down to me for examination and appraisal and my pleasure in them made them even more precious to Granny.

She herself was a small, plump woman who must have been petite and very pretty. She was always dressed in black – boots, woollen stockings, overall – a dark, inelegant black, turning grey with too much washing and too much exposure to the weather. But above the neck, she was a surprise of strong colour: white hair, sea-blue eyes, and a quick, fresh face, tanned deep with sun. When something delighted her, she had a habit of wagging her head rapidly from side to side like a precocious child with ringlets and, although she was over sixty then, she behaved like a woman half that age. Indeed, when I felt tired or lazy and she would challenge me to race her to the byre or dare me to go beyond her along the rocks at low water, I used to tell her that she was 'nothing but a giddy, feather-headed old woman,' repeating what I had heard my mother say of her so often.

Even on the best day in summer, Mullaghduff is a desolate place. The land is rocky, barren, uneven, covered by a brown heather that never blooms and hacked into a crazy jigsaw by hundreds of tiny rivulets no more than a foot wide which seemed to flow in as many different directions and yet cunningly avoid crossing one another. Granny's house lay at the most inaccessible end of this vast waste, three miles from the nearest road. It was a strange place to make a home but Grandfather was a dour, silent man and he probably felt that by marrying the girl of seventeen who had an infant daughter but no father to claim it, he had shown sufficient charity: the least she could do was accept the terms of his proposal. Or perhaps he was jealous of her vivacity and attractiveness and thought that the wide Atlantic behind her and a three-mile stretch of moor before her would be good deterrents to a roaming spirit. Whatever his motives, he succeeded in cutting her off so completely from the world that at the time of her death, shortly after my thirteenth birthday, the longest jouney she had ever made was to the town of Strabane, fifty-two miles away, and that journey she had made the month before her marriage to fix up legal documents in connection with her baby, my mother.

She and I had riotous times together. We laughed with one another and at one another. (A constant source of fun was Granny's English. Gaelic was her first tongue and she never felt at ease in English which she shouted and spat out as if it were getting in her way.) We used to sit up until near midnight, chatting and gossiping, and then instead of going to bed, perhaps decide suddenly to feast ourselves on herring fried in butter or on sand eels roasted on the red coals or on a wild duck that was for the next day's dinner. Or we would huddle round the fire and I would read to her stories from my school reading-book – she could neither read nor write. She would listen avidly to these, her face keen with interest, not missing a word, making me go back over a paragraph which she did not fully understand or halting me with a question about some detail in the story.

'Were you in a bus ever? A real bus – for people?'

'Once.'

'What was it like, what? Was it bad on the stomach, was it?'

Or after reading, she herself would retell the story to me ('Just to see did I understand it right') especially if it was a tale about the daring of the lighthouse-keeper's daughter or a cameo biography of someone like Madame Curie or Florence Nightingale. And then the greed for knowledge about the outside world would fall away as quickly from her and she would jump to her feet and say, 'Christ; son, we near forgot!' She used this swear word without any suggestion of profanity and because, I believe now, she rarely heard the conversation of women of her own time. 'If we run to the lower rocks, we'll see the Norwegian fishing boats going round the point. Hurry, son, hurry! They're a sight on a good night. Hurry!'

Out there on the rump of Mullaghduff she had no ready-made entertainments to amuse me, but she thought nothing of her own discomfort to make my stay with her more interesting. We often rose before dawn to see wild geese spearing through the icy air high above the ocean. Or we sat for hours at a stretch on the flat rocks below her house to get a glimpse of sharks encircling an oily patch that betrayed a shoal of mackerel and then attacking it. Or we waded knee-deep in water at the shallow strand and felt the terrible thrill of fluke wriggling beneath our bare feet, closed our eyes and plunged our hands down to lift them out. I know now that all these little expeditions were thought up to amuse me but I am also certain that, once we had embarked on them, Granny enjoyed them every bit as much as I did.

'Christ, it's a calf I have under my foot and not a fluke at all!' she would squeal with nervous delight, her blue eyes radiant with joy. 'Come here, son! Come here and steady the arm of me!'

Or if we were standing on top of the hump of ground behind her house to get a good view of a passing transatlantic liner, all sequins of lights, she would fill it for me with a passenger list of gay, carefree people: 'Lords and ladies,' she would say. 'The men of them handsome and straight as heroes and the women of them in bright silks down to their toes and all of them laughing and dancing and drinking wine and singing. Christ, son, but they're a happy old cargo!'

There was a February gale blowing in from the sea the evening the packman battled his way up to us. I watched him through the kitchen window, a shrub in the middle of the bog, only it was bending against the wind. Then it grew to a man and then a man with a cardboard case half as big as himself. When he was a stone's throw from the door, I saw that he was coloured. In those days, packmen were fairly common in remote areas. They went from house to house with their packs or cases of clothes and socks and bed linens and table cloths and gaudy knick-knacks and if a customer had no money for the goods chosen, the packmen were usually willing to settle for the value in poultry or fish. They had the name of being sharp dealers, dishonest even.

The sight of this packman put the fear of God in me because mother had taught us to be wary of all packmen and I had never seen a coloured man before in my life. I led Granny to the window and peeped out from behind her.

'Will he attack us?' I whimpered.

'Christ and if he does, he'll meet his match in this house!' she said bravely and threw open the door. 'Come in, lad,' she roared into the storm. 'Come and rest yourself, for no goat could have made the climb up here today but a fool like yourself.'

He backed into the kitchen, dragging his huge case after him. He dropped into a chair at the door and his head fell back to a resting position against the wall. His breath came in quick, short gasps and he made no effort to speak, he was so exhausted.

I took a step closer to him to examine him. He was a young man, no more than twenty, with a smooth, hazel skin that was a tight fit for his face. The crown of his head was swathed in a snow-white turban, wound round like a bandage. His shoulders were narrow, his body puny, his trousers frayed and wet from the long grass, and his feet as small as my younger sister's. Then I saw his hands. They were fine and delicate and the fingers tipped with pink nails as polished as fresh seaweed. On the third finger of his left hand was a ring. It was a gold ring, wrought in imitation of a snake which held between its mouth and tail a damson-coloured stone. As I watched it, the colour became vaporous, like smoke in a bottle, and seemed to writhe languidly in a coiling movement. Now it was purple, now rose, now black, now blood-red, now blue, now the colour of sloes in the August sun. I was still gazing at its miracles when the packman slid to his knees on the ground and began reciting in a low, droning voice, 'I sell beau-ti-ful things, good lady; everything to adorn your beau-ti-ful home. What is it you buy? Leenens, silks, sheets, beau-ti-ful pictures for your walls, beau-ti-ful cardigans for the lady. What is it you buy?'

As he spoke, he opened his case and removed all its contents, painting the floor with yellows and greens and whites and blues. He did not offer any one item but displayed everything as if for his own gratification – and no wonder, for he owned all the riches of the earth.

'You buy, good lady? What is it you buy?' he intoned without interest, without enthusiasm, but by rote, because he was tired beyond caring. His eyes never left the ground and his hands spread the splashes of colour out and around him until he was an island in a lake of brightness.

For a moment, Granny said nothing. She was dazzled by the packman's wares and at the same time she was trying desperately not to miss whatever it was he was saying and his accent was difficult for her. When at last words came to her, they broke from her in a sort of cry.

'Aw, Christ, sweet Christ, look at them! Look at them! Aw, God, what is there like them things!' Then rapidly to me, 'What is he saying, son, what? Tell me what it is he's saying.' Then to the packman, 'Mister, I don't speak English too good, mister. Aw, Christ, mister, but they're grand treasures, mister, grand.'

She dropped to the floor beside him and stretched her hands out as if in benediction over the goods. Then her arms went gently down and the tips of her fingers brushed over the surfaces of the garments. She went silent with awe and her mouth opened. Only her eyes were quick with ecstasy.

'Try them on, good lady. Sample what I have to sell.'

She turned to me to confirm that she had heard correctly.

'Put on the things you like,' I said. 'Go ahead.'

She looked at the packman, searching his face to see was he in earnest, fearful in case he was not.

'I have no money, Mister Packman. No money.'

As if she had not spoken, the packman went on rearranging his colours and did not look up. Only routine was carrying him through.

'Try them on. They are beau-ti-ful. All.'

She hesitated momentarily, poised over the limitless choice.

'Go on,' I said impatiently. 'Hurry up.'

'Everything for the good lady and for her home,' mumbled the packman to the ground. 'Sample what I have to sell.'

She swooped on them as if she were going to devour them. Her fingers found a scarlet blouse which she snatched up and held against her chest. She looked down at it, looked to us for approbation, held it under her chin and smoothed it out against her, while her other hand went instinctively to her hair which she gathered back from her face. Then she was absolutely still, waiting for our verdict.

'Beau-ti-ful,' mumbled the packman automatically.

'Beautiful,' I said, anxious to have everything sampled and done with.

'Beautiful,' echoed Granny, softly, slowly, as if she were using the word for the first time.

Then suddenly she was on her feet, towering above us and leaping around the kitchen floor in a wild, mocking dance. 'Christ!' she squealed. 'Youse would have me as silly in the head as the two of youse are. Look at me! Look at me! Fit for a palace I am, in all my grandeur!'

Then she cut loose altogether. She flung the blouse to the floor and seized a yellow mohair stole which she draped around her shoulders and paraded up and down the floor in time to her own singing. Then she tried on a green hat and then white gloves and then a blue cardigan and then a multicoloured apron, all the time singing or dancing or waving her arms, all the time shaking her head like mad, delighted, embarrassed, drunk with pleasure, completely carried away.

Before she had gone through half of the garments, the years put an end to her antics and she flung herself exhausted on top of the bed and let herself go limp. 'Now, mister, you can take the bloody load away,' she panted, 'for I have no money to buy anything.'

Again the packman did not hear her but shuffled his goods with weary patience and said in his dressy way, 'This you like, good lady.' He touched a pair of brass candlesticks. 'Beau-ti-ful. Very cheap. Very, very cheap.' Granny waved her hands in dismissal.

'No money, Mister. No money.'

'Or you like this, good lady, this beau-ti-ful picture of the Holy Divine Redeemer. Also very cheap to you, good lady.'

She closed her eyes and shook her head and waited for her energy to return.

'A lovely thing this, kind lady.' His hand happened on a tiny box covered with imitation leather. Inside lay half a dozen apostle spoons. 'These I sell by large numbers. Everybody loved them. I cannot get them enough,' he said without conviction. 'The box to you, good lady, for half price.'

'Shut up!' she snapped with sudden venom, springing up to a sitting position on the bed and scattering the languor that had emanated from the dealer. 'Shut up, Packman! We are poor people here! We have nothing! Shut up!'

The packman's head sank lower to the ground and he began gathering his goods in to him. It was dark now and he fumbled with the catch on his case.

She regretted her outburst at once because she hopped off the bed and began building up the peat fire. 'You'll eat with us, Packman; there'll be hunger on you. We can offer you . . . ' She paused and swung round to me. 'Christ, son, we'll roast the grouse that was to be Sunday's dinner! That's what we'll do. Grouse and praties and butter and buttermilk and soda farls – a feast, by Christ, a feast!' She turned to the packman. 'Can your stomach hold a feast, Packman?'

'Anything, good lady. Anything.'

'A feast it'll be then,' she pronounced. 'A feast and be damned to Sunday.'

She rolled up her sleeves and began setting the table. The packman closed his case and went to a corner where he merged with the dark.

'Tell me, Packman,' she called to him from her work. 'What do they call you, what?'

'Singh,' he said.

'What?'

'Singh,' he repeated.

'Man, but that's a strange name. Sing. Sing,' she said, feeling the sound on her tongue. 'I'll tell you what I'll call you, Packman,' she went on, 'I'll call you Mr Sing My Heart's Delight! That's what I'll call you – a good, big mouthful. Mr Sing My Heart's Delight!'

'Yes,' he said submissively.

'Now, Mr Sing My Heart's Delight, let the sleep come over you for an hour and when I give you the call, there'll be a feast and a festival before your eyes. Close your eyes and sleep, you poor battered man, you.'

He closed his eyes obediently and within five minutes his head had fallen on his chest.

We ate by the light of an oil lamp, Granny at the bottom of the table, me in the middle, and the packman in the place of honour at the top. It must have been a month since he had a square meal because he bolted his food ravenously and did not lift his eyes until his plate was cleaned. Then he sat back in his seat and smiled at us for the first time. He looked boyish now that he was sated.

'Thank you, good lady,' he said. 'A beau-ti-ful meal.'

'You're welcome,' she said. 'May none of us ever want.' She held the bone of the grouse's leg between her fingers and drew patterns on her plate, her head to one side.

'Where do you come from, Mr Sing My Heart's Delight?' Her tone suggested she was beginning a series of questions.

'The Punjab,' he said.

'And where might that be?'

'India, good lady.'

'India,' she repeated. 'Tell me, is India a hot country, is it?'

'Very warm. Very warm and very poor.'

'Very poor,' she said quietly, adding the detail to the picture she was composing in her mind. 'And the oranges and the bananas grow there on trees and there are all classes of fruit and flowers with all the colours of the rainbow in them?'

'Yes,' he said simply, for he was remembering his own picture. 'It is very beau-ti-ful, good lady. Very beau-ti-ful.'

'And the women,' Granny went on, 'do they wear long silk frocks melting down to the ground? And the men, are the men dressed in claret velvet and black shoes with silver buckles?'

He spread his hands and smiled.

'And the women, strolling about in the sun under the orange-trees and the sun taking lights out of their hair and the gallant men raising their feathered hats to them and stepping off the roads to let them pass . . . in the sun . . . in the Punjab . . . in the Garden of Eden . . .' She was away from us as she spoke, leaving us in the draughty, flagged-floor kitchen, listening to the wind ripping up the ocean below us and trying the weaker parts of the thatched roof. The packman's eyes were closed and his head nodded.

'The Garden of Eden,' said Granny again. 'Where the ground isn't treacherous with bits of streams and the land so rocky that even weeds won't settle in it. And you have God's sun in that Punjab place and there is singing and the playing of musical instruments and the children . . . aye, the children . . . ' The first drops of a shower came down the chimney and sizzled in the fire.

'Christ!' she said, springing to her feet. 'What class of dottering fools of men am I talking to? Up you get, you clowns you, and let me get at the washing-up.'

The packman woke with a start and made for his case.

'And where are you going?' she shouted to him. 'Christ, man, a badger wouldn't face out on a night like this!'

He stopped in the middle of the floor.

'Well?' she said. 'Don't look at me as if you expected a beating. You'll sleep here tonight. There – across the front of the fire. Like a cat,' she ended off with a shout of laughter.

The packman laughed too.

'Now Mr Sing My Heart's Delight, get out of my road until me and my wee man here gets cleared up.'

By the time we had the dishes finished and fresh peat spread before the fire for the morning, it was bedtime. Granny and I slept together in the bed in the corner, a huge iron bed whose side was always warm from the hearth. She lay next to the wall and I on the outside. Now we retreated to the shadowy end of the room and undressed. Then, with a skip and a jump, we were in bed together before the packman had time to be embarrassed.

Granny peeped across me. 'Blow out the lamp, Mr Sing My Heart's Delight, and then place yourself on the floor there. You'll find a mat at the door if you want it.'

'Good night, good lady,' he said. 'Very good lady.'

'Good night, Mr Sing My Heart's Delight,' she replied.

He got the mat and stretched himself out before the red and white embers. Outside, the rain lashed against the roof and, inside, the three of us were as cosy as pet hens.

It was a fine morning, a fresh, blustering day that kept the clouds moving past and dried the path that led from the house to the main road. The packman was young and bright and his case seemed lighter too because he swung it easily by his side as he stood at the door, nodding his head and smiling happily as Granny directed him towards the parishes where he would have the best chance to sell his wares.

'And now,' she said in conclusion, 'God's speed and may the road rise with you.'

'To pay you I have no money, good lady,' said the packman, 'and my worthless goods I would not offer you because . . .'

'Off with you, man. Off with you. There'll be rain before dinnertime and you should have eight miles behind you by then.' The packman still hesitated. He kept smiling and bowing and swinging his case as if he were a shy girl.

'Christ, Mr Sing My Heart's Delight, if you don't soon go, it's here you'll be for dinner and you ate it last night!'

The packman put his case on the ground and looked at his left hand. Then, drawing off the ring with those long, delicate fingers of his, he held it forward towards her. 'For you,' he said, in a very formal voice. 'Please accept from me in . . . in grateful.'

Even as it lay on his hand, the stone turned a dozen colours. Granny was embarrassed. It had been so long since she had been offered a present that she did not know how to accept it. She hung her head and muttered churlishly, 'No. No. No,' and backed away from the gift.

'But please, good lady. Please,' the packman insisted. 'From a Punjab gentleman to a Donegal lady. A present. Please.'

When she did not come forward to accept it, he moved towards her and caught her hand in his. He chose the third finger of the left hand and slipped the ring on it. 'Thank you, good lady,' he said.

Then he lifted his case, bowed to us again and turned towards the barren waste and the main road. The wind was behind him and carried him quickly away.

Neither of us moved until we had lost him behind the hillock at the bend of the road. I turned to go round to the side of the house: it was time to let the hens out and milk the cow. But Granny did not move. She stood looking towards the road with her arm and hand still held as the packman had left them.

'Come on, Granny,' I said irritably. 'The cow will think we're dead.'

She looked strangely at me and then away from me and across the bogs and the road and up towards the mountains which almost surrounded her.

'Come on, Granny,' I said, tugging at her overall. 'Come on. Come on.'

She allowed me to pull her; and as I led her towards the byre, I heard her saying to herself, 'I'm thinking the rain will get him this side of Crolly Bridge and the claret breeches and the buckled shoes will be destroyed on him. Please God it will make a good day of it. Please God it will.'

All Fall Down

HELEN LUCY BURKE 1980

The girl in this story is deeply ashamed of her alcoholic father. She tries to avoid public embarrassment, especially on the important occasion of her Confirmation. Her parents support her in keeping up public appearances but it is not enough to evade disaster.

There was not an ounce of innate prejudice against me in the heart of Miss O'Leary. Every now and then she took us on 'Nature Walks' to point us out interesting weeds and mushrooms that would clarify the botanical bits in our reader. In the same way she used me and my family to illustrate her thesis on alcohol.

By disposition she was very strong against the drink. The parish priest urged her to still greater extremities of zeal – our parish was a horror for alcohol. Who could blame her for her enthusiasm when daily, opposite her very window, she was presented with a text-book example?

Who but me?

Each day at half-past two came my moment of torture: for that was the time when my father, chased out of the pub for the regulation hour, went staggering home past the windows of the school.

'See, children,' Miss O'Leary would cry, all professional interest, 'how alcohol depresses the brain, causing loss of muscular control.'

My father was a long, thin man. His legs wobbled about as awkwardly as the legs of a newly-dropped colt. There was a bit of a rise in the boreen outside the school, and there he always fell. It used to take him a long time to get up. He would throw one leg out in front of him, stiff as the fork of a compass: but then the other leg pivoted away, and there he was again, sprawling in the mud. His face was very calm and serious all the time. None of us ever attempted to help him. Miss O'Leary instructed us that drunks had terrible tempers and that we were not to trust ourselves near them, any more than we would go beside a ram or a bull.

Of course the other kids had fathers who got drunk – there was not an abstainer in the whole parish – but they did it in a jollier way altogether, at fairs and card-parties: and afterwards they went home and beat the tar out of

On the Terrace by Terence P. Flanagan

their wives and children, which was thought nicer and more natural.

Basically, the great local failing was not alcohol but excess. The women never touched a drop of fermented liquor, but instead got their release in exaggerated fervour of church-going. They practised bowings before the altar, daily Communion, weekly Confession at which they accused themselves of interesting faults like over-zealousness and scruples, and all sorts of other religious *bonne-bouches* in the style of Sodalities and Leagues against Swearing. At night while their husbands were out drinking and gambling, they cautioned their huge families against marriage and did their best to turn their minds in the direction of monasteries and nunneries.

Among this crew my father was an oddity. He did not beat my mother or me. He drank alone. He showed no loud enjoyment of his drink – poor man, what was wine to them was blood to him. Worst of all he was a sort of gentleman, and the wrong sort, the quiet standoffish kind. If he had turned out for the first meet of the season and galloped his half-mile with the hounds there would have been no animosity. Even attendance now and then at a point-to-point would have been better than nothing.

Quite simply, I hated him. At night, lying with the blankets drawn over my head and tucked in the far side of the pillow, I used to scheme how I would kill him before I was eighteen. A push down the stairs from the top landing – now that would be a fine thing!

Most of the time I think he did not know I was there. If by chance he noticed me, I embarrassed him so much that he gave me all his loose change.

One night, coming home from the village, my father was knocked down by a straying cow who rolled him into the ditch. There he lay, all the freezing night. When he was found the next morning his condition was grave. My mother had him conveyed to the hospital forty miles away. So that she might be free to sit at his bedside – his death was expected – she sent me by train to Dublin as a boarder in a convent school. I believe she was quite fond of him.

I was ten years old.

For the next two days I cried steadily, more because it was expected of me than from grief. After this purge I settled down into the bliss of a life that I could build to my own specifications.

There are strange paradises in this world. Mine was compounded of long dark corridors smelling of paraffin polish and disinfectant, a playground paved with cinders, staircases hollowed out of the mouldering walls, a corner of the nuns' garden where we dug plots for seeds.

Oh, the strangeness of the customs! The nuns bowed as they passed each other in the corridors. If they were alone they swept down the middle of the passages, majestic in their white starched bonnets as ships in full sail; and we pupils crowded in against the walls and bowed humbly with hands folded. Impassive, they never returned our reverences but floated rapidly on, their faces adorned with little mysterious smiles.

They filled me with awe. Nature must have moulded them from a different clay. Surely they were not of the same make as the harried red and brown women of Kilanore. I remember my horror when one day, peeping from a forbidden window, I saw the nuns' knickers hanging like great white spinnakers from the clothes-line. I told my infamy later in Confession.

We went to bed at nine o'clock and we rose at six. Once a month we had a bath. Hair-washing was not permitted for the whole length of the term. Some abandoned girls secretly used to wash their hair after the lights were out, and dried it on their pillows; but we were told that God had His eyes on them and sooner or later He would punish them by striking them deaf.

A number of the girls had lice. When this was spotted – we were watched pretty sharply for undue scatching – they were combed over an enamel basin with a fine comb dipped in paraffin. For weeks these victims went round smelling of paraffin and howling for grief that their shame had been exposed.

All this was paradise because my father was not near. In fact, I spread it around that I had no father. Died while I was small, I said, and basked in the caressing sympathy of the older girls.

I never heard from him, of course, and when my mother wrote it was just dry little notes saying that things were going well, or things could be better, or things were not so well. The nuns opened the letters and read them before we got them, but that did not disturb me. I did not even wonder what would happen if they got to hear of my fictions. Life was taking place on two planes, and the plane of the imagination was the more real. Religion helped. Sin was all around us, we were told, lurking like a worm at the heart of an apple, invisible until you got to the ruined core. Opportunities for virtue were offered as plentifully. At lunch in the refectory one day Frances Boylan got a decayed human tooth in her stew. She wept and complained, but the refectarian pointed out the great opportunity she had missed for gaining grace by 'offering it up' and saying nothing. Next day they read to us from the 'Lives of the Saints' about a French lady who developed her sanctity by eating spits off the ground.

Heaven lay about us, and so did Hell, and the school was an infinite wonder, a battleground of forces contending for possession of us; and yet pure, unsensual, unworldly, a place where everything including sin could take place in the mind.

Kilanore and its grossness became a memory.

Easter came, making a dent in the routine. Christ died. Prayer-books banged with sinister noise in the darkened chapel at Tenebrae. He rose again from the dead. We were allowed to attend three Masses on Easter Sunday. Afterwards there were boiled eggs for breakfast, and in the afternoon there was a film about the Missions. A number of girls, including myself, did not go home for the Easter holidays. We all cried a little each night, and the other girls petted me and stroked me because my father was dead and I was so brave. Frances Boylan, who was two months older than me, said she would be my best friend. The sun shone and my whole body seemed to blossom and to send out green shoots. I knew at last that God lived and loved me.

I prepared with fervour for my Confirmation.

Not long after term started again my mother wrote to say that himself was out of hospital. The two of them planned to attend my Confirmation.

It was my sentence of death.

Closing my eyes tightly to shut out the pictures that presented themselves I could see them all the more clearly. My father lurching over the parquet floor . . . the fall and the sprawl and the dreadful efforts to get up . . . the girls turning kindly away so as not to see and not to know that I had lied.

I wrote to him for the first time in my life, told him what I had done, and demanded that he stay his distance. A few days later I got a letter from my mother saying that she and my uncle would be arriving for the Confirmation.

I had no uncle.

We walked – no, proceeded – slowly up the aisle, heads bent in reverence. Our white dresses creaked over layers of petticoats. The weather had turned cold, but none of us wore a coat that might hide the glory of our rows of picot-edged frills. Frances Boylan beside me had only four rows of frills: I had six, and this was a triumph that made me love her even more. When the Bishop tapped us on the cheek with a withered hand that rustled like paper she grabbed my arm and held it tightly, not daring to look up, while I stared boldly into the beaky face, lemon-coloured under the mitre, and the Bishop stared back at me the way an angry cock does.

Later, we promised to abide by the truths of our religion and to refrain from alcohol under the age of twenty-one. We chorused this in unison, and no voice was stronger than mine.

Parents and children met afterwards in the Middle Parlour. Awkwardly, on the chill expanse of waxed parquet, the family groups talked in low embarrassed voices. Even Frances Boylan's father, who was a stout red-faced bookmaker, planed the rough race-course edges off his voice and fluted out his conversation in a genteel treble.

My father seemed at ease. He did not come forward to meet me but stood quietly waiting, as if he were ready to be disowned without making a fuss.

My mother and he kissed me. I noticed at once that he did not smell of drink. There was a carnation in the buttonhole of his suit. It was a new suit, dark-brown fine tweed with a little hair in it that scratched my cheek when he pressed me against him.

'Your uncle came out of hospital a fortnight ago,' said my mother.

I nodded my head politely up and down. 'I hope you're better,' I said.

'Not too bad.' He spoke in a sort of ghost voice, that seemed to come with great effort from a great distance. His face had got smaller and was a funny clear colour, a bit like the tracing paper we used for making maps, but greyer. His moustache was gone, so that it was easier to see his mouth, and to see that his lips trembled slightly but continually. Each time he caught my eye he tried to smile, but could not quite make it. I left them and went to the table where tea and sandwiches and seedcake were set out.

Frances Boylan and Una Sheedy asked me was that my uncle.

'It is,' I said. 'He's just after coming out of hospital.'

'He's lovely looking,' said Frances. Flabbergasted, I realised that she meant it; and that she was comparing his emaciated elegance with her stout common father. And I realised that she too was ashamed of her father. Did all children hate their parents, I wondered? It seemed a new strong bond. I led them over to be introduced.

'This is my mother and my Uncle Matthew,' I said.

He stood up at once and shook hands. Then he asked their permission to smoke. Reverent in their awe for his politeness they assured him that they did not mind. My mother stood in the background with a shut-off expression on her face. Presently she said that they must go. My father gave me a five- pound note, and bowed to Una and Frances.

We left the parlour all five of us together, like a family, or like a herd of does with the stag. No, that was not it either, for he deferred to us so lightly and gently that it was more like a king with a group of young queens, his equals in rank, but younger.

Worshipping, Frances and Una, drifted forward beside him, while my mother and I as proprietors hung back a little and let them have their fill. He told them to call him uncle, and they did so. He took the carnation from his buttonhole and presented it to them jointly, regretting that roses were not in season. We came to the head of the marble stairs. Frances and Una drew back, I moved forward to escort my visitors down to the door.

The saints smiled at us from the walls. He turned back to wave to my friends and his footing went. His stick tumbled before him down to the foot of the stairs. Behind it he rolled, threshing with his arms for a hold to save himself. There was a dull sound from each stair as he struck, then silence when he reached the bottom. We stared down at him, an insect on its back, waving its legs. There was no power in them, like tentacles they moved. His head came up several times and turned vaguely about.

'He's killed,' screamed Frances and Una. They started down the stairs. I ran past them and picked up his stick.

It took the combined strength of my mother and two nuns to get me away from him. As I struck, his eyes looked up at me for each blow and winced away as the stick fell. He said nothing, although his mouth writhed. He did not cry out.

They sent me to the sickroom with hot milk and aspirin. Later the priest came. He sat at the end of my bed for a long time. All I would say in answer to his questioning was: 'He fell down again.'

A few weeks later I got word that my father had died. It was alcohol poisoning, I learned later.

Nuns at Prayer by Reverend Jack P. Hanlon (pencil and watercolour on paper)

The Wrong Vocation

MOY McCRORY 1990

To have a vocation is to feel a deep and serious commitment to a particular walk of life; it could be to medicine, to teaching, or to the Church. Among Irish Catholics, wherever they may live, it nearly always refers to the religious life of a priest or a nun and it is understood as a call from the spirit of God. In spite of her light-hearted approach to life, the Liverpool girl who tells this story knows that to refuse this Call is a terrible thing. She has a nightmarish picture of this vocation swooping down on her and she does everything she can to escape it.

'When God calls you, he is never denied,' Sister Mercy told us with a finality which struck terror into our hearts.

She stood at the front of the room with the window behind her, so we were blinded and could not see her features but we knew she smiled.

'He waits patiently until we hear His voice. When that happens, you are never the same.'

It terrified me when this thing called a vocation might come; any day out of nowhere to drop into my mind and wedge there like a piece of grit.

'God is looking now, seeing who is pure of heart and ready to be offered up.'

Every girl shifted uncomfortably. Sister looked at our upturned faces and seemed pleased with the effect she was having. By way of illustration she told us about a young woman from a rich home who was always laughing, with young men waiting to escort her here, there and everywhere, and a big family house with chandeliers in the rooms and a lake in the garden.

'I've seen it. It was on the telly the other night,' Nancy Lyons whispered to me.

'With all these good things in life, she was spoiled. Her wealthy father indulged his daughter's every wish. And do you think she was happy?'

'She damned well ought to be,' Nancy hissed while around us the more pious members of the form shook their heads.

Sister placed her bony hands across her chest and stood up on her tiptoes as if reaching with her ribcage for something that would constantly evade it.

'Her heart was empty.'

Sister went on to tell us how the young woman resisted the call, but eventually realised she would never be happy until she devoted her life to Christ. Going out beside the lake, she asked him to enter her life.

'She is one of our very own nuns, right here in this convent. Of course I cannot tell you which sister she is, but when you imagine that we were all born as nuns, remember that we were once young girls like yourselves, without a thought in our heads that we should devote our lives to God.'

There was a silence. We all stared out past her head.

'Oh Sister, it's beautiful,' said a voice. Nancy rolled her eyes to heaven. Lumpy, boring Beatrice, who always sat at the front, would like it. She was so slow-witted and so good. She was one of the least popular girls in the class, a reporter of bad news and always the first to give homework in. With mini-skirts *de rigueur*, her uniform remained stoically unadapted. She must have been the only girl in the school that did not need to have her hemline checked at the end of the day. While we struggled to turn over our waistbands Beatrice always wore her skirt a good two inches below her plump knees and looked like one of the early photographs, all sepia and foggy, of the old girls in their heyday.

Nancy pulled her face.

'But wasn't her rich father angry?' someone asked, and Sister Mercy nodded.

'Mine would sodding kill me. They don't even want me to stay on at school. Me mother's always reminding me how much money they're losing because I'm not bringing any wages home.'

'Do you have something to say, Nancy Lyons?' Sister's stern voice rapped.

'No Sister, I was just saying what a great sacrifice it was to make.'

'Ah yes, a great sacrifice indeed.'

But the sacrifice was not just on the nun's part. Everyone else was made to suffer. There was a woman in our street who never recovered after her eldest daughter joined the Carmelites. Mrs Roddy's daughter was a teacher in the order. It was not so much that she would never give her mother grandchildren that caused the greatest upset, but the economics of it where all a nun's earnings go straight back into the convent. Mrs Roddy used to wring her hands.

'That money's mine,' she would shout, 'for feeding and clothing her all those years. The church has no right to it!'

Then her daughter went peculiar. We only noticed because they sent her home for a week on holiday, and we thought that was unusual, but it was around the time they were relaxing the rule. Nuns were appearing on the streets with skirts that let them walk easily, skimming their calves instead of the pavement.

During that week she got her cousin to perm her hair, on account of the new headdress. She assured her that it was all right because even nuns had to look groomed now their hair showed at the front, and every night she continued to lead the family in the joyful mysteries.

'I'll tell you Mrs Mac, I'm worn out with all the praying since our Delcia's been back,' her mother would confide to mine as they passed quickly in the street, while her daughter muttered 'God bless you' to no one in particular and with a vague smile into the air.

But indoors, she borrowed her mother's lipstick, deep red because Mrs Roddy still had the same one from before the war. That was when they thought she was going a bit far, when they saw her outmoded, crimson mouth chanting the rosary. She drove her family mad. She had tantrums and kept slamming doors. Then they saw her out in the street asking to be taken for rides on Nessie Moran's motorbike. Everyone said she had taken her vows too young. She crammed all those teenage things she never did into that week. By the end of it they were relieved to send her back.

Her mother hated nuns. She did not mind priests half as much.

'At least they're human,' she would say. 'Well, half human. Nuns aren't people; they're not proper women. They don't know what it is to be a mother and they'll never be high up in the church. They'll never be the next Pope. They can't even say Mass. What good are they? They're stuck in the middle, not one thing or the other. Brides of Christ! They make me sick. Let them try cooking, cleaning and running a home on nothing. It would be a damned easier life I'd have if I'd married Christ, instead of that lazy bugger inside.'

But she was fond of the young priest at her church, a good-looking, fresh-faced man from Antrim who would sit and have a drink with them at the parish club.

'At least you can have a laugh with him,' she'd say, 'but that stuck-up lot, they're all po-faced up at Saint Ursula's. They're no better than any of us. I'm a woman, don't I know what their minds are like. We're no different. Gossipy, unnatural creatures, those ones are. Look what's happened to our poor Delcia after being with them.'

And then the convent sent Delcia home to be looked after by her family. An extended holiday, they called it, on account of her stress and exhaustion.

'They've used her up, now they don't want what's left over, so I've got her again. What good is she to anyone now? She can't look after herself. She can't even make a bloody cup of tea. How will she fend for herself if the order won't have her back. I'm dying, Mrs Mac, I can't be doing with her.'

My mother would tut and nod and shut the door.

'It's a shame. What sort of life has that poor girl had?' she would say indoors, shaking her head at the tragedy.

'I know she's gone soft now, but she was good at school. Her mam and dad thought she'd be something and now she's fit for nothing if the church can't keep her.'

In the evening we would hear Mrs Roddy shouting, 'Get in off the street!'

Finally they took her into a hospice and we heard no more about it, but Mrs Roddy always crossed the road to avoid nuns. Once outside Lewis's a Poor Clare thrust a collection box at her and asked for a donation. Mrs Roddy tried to take it from her and the box was pulled back and forth like a bird tugging at a worm. It was not the nun's iron grip, but the bit of elastic which wrapped itself around her wrist that foiled Mrs Roddy's attempt to redistribute the church's wealth.

'They're just like vultures,' she would say, 'waiting to see what they can tear from your limbs. They're only happy when they've picked you clean. Better hide your purse!'

At the collection on Sundays she sat tight-lipped and the servers knew better than to pass the collecting plate her way.

'A vocation gone wrong' was what my father called Delcia Roddy. He would shake his head from side to side and murmur things like 'the shame' or 'the waste'. He had a great deal of sympathy for her tortured soul. It was about this time that I became tortured. He had no sympathy for me.

Sister Mercy's words had stung like gravel in a grazed knee. At night I could hear them as her voice insisted, 'You cannot fight God's plan,' and I would pray that God keep his plans to himself.

'You must pray for a vocation,' she told us.

I gritted my teeth and begged his blessed mother to intervene.

'I'll be worse than the Roddy girl,' I threatened, 'and look what a disgrace she was.' Then, echoing the epitaph of W. B. Yeats, I would point in the darkness and urge 'Horseman, pass by!'

It was rather the reverse of the chosen people who daubed their doorposts and let the angel of death pass over, in order to survive and play out God's plan. I wanted God's plan to pass over.

'We are instruments in God's will,' Sister Mercy told us and I did not want to be an instrument.

I knew if God had any sense he would not want me, but Sister Mercy frightened us. Beatrice was the one headed for a convent. She had made plain her intentions at the last retreat when she stood up and announced to the study group that she was thinking of devoting her life to Christ.

'She may as well, there's nothing else down for her,' Nancy commented.

Yet Sister Mercy told us that it was the ones we did not suspect who had vocations, and she had looked around the room like a mind reader scrutinising the audience before pulling out likely candidates.

The convent terrified me; the vocation stalked my shadow like a store detective. One day it would pounce and I would be deadlocked into a religious life, my will subsumed by one greater than I. Up there was a rapacious appetite which consumed whole lives, like chicken legs. I dreaded that I should end up in a place where every day promised the same, the gates locked behind me and all other escape sealed off. It wasn't that I had any ambitions for what I might do, but I could not happily reconcile myself to an existence where the main attraction was death. I dreaded hearing God's call.

'He can spend years. He can wait. God is patient.'

I decided that I would have to exasperate him, and fast.

Down at the Pier Head, pigeons gathered in thousands. The Liver Buildings were obscured by their flight when they all rose in unison like a blanket of grey and down. I never knew where my fear came from, but I was terrified of those birds. Harmless seagulls twice their size flew about me, followed the ferry out across the water to Birkenhead and landed flapping and breathless on the landing plank. Their screech was piercing, and they never disturbed me. Yet when I stepped out into Hamilton Square and saw the tiny cluster of city birds waiting, my heart would beat in panic. City birds who left slime where they went, their excrement the colour of the new granite buildings springing up. They nodded their heads and watched you out of the sides of their eyes. They knocked smaller birds out of the way and I had seen them taking bread away from each other. They were a fighting, quarrelsome brood, an untidy shambling army, with nothing to do all day but walk around the Pier Head or follow me through Princess Park and make my life a misery.

Once I was crossing for a bus just as a streak of them flew up into the air. I put my hands over my head, the worst fear being that one should touch my face, and I could think of nothing more sickening than the feel of one of these ragged creatures, bloated with disease; the flying vermin which flocked around the Life Assurance building, to remind us we were mortal.

A nightmare I had at the time was of being buried alive under thousands of these birds. They would make that strange cooing noise as they slowly suffocated me. Their fat greasy bodies would pulsate and swell as, satiated, they nestled down on to me for the heat my body could provide. Under this sweltering, stinking mass I would be unable to scream. Each time I opened my mouth it filled with dusty feathers.

Then my nightmare changed. Another element crept into my dreams. Alongside the pigeons crept the awful shape that was a vocation. It came in all colours, brown and white, black and white, beige, mottled, grey and sandy, as the different robes of each order clustered around me, knocking pigeons out of the way. They muttered snatches of Latin, bits of psalms, and rubbed their claw-like hands together like bank tellers. The big change in the dream was that they, unlike the pigeons, did not suffocate me, but slowly drew away, leaving me alone in a great empty space, that at first I thought was the bus terminal, but which Nancy Lyons assured me was the image of my life to be.

Her older sister read tea leaves and was very interested in dreams. Nancy borrowed a book from her.

'It says here that dreaming about water means a birth.'

'I was dreaming about pigeons, and then nuns.'

'Yeah, but you said you were down at the Pier Head, didn't you, and that's water.'

'I don't know if I was at the Pier Head.'

'Oh you must have been. Where else would you get all them pigeons?' Nancy was a realist. 'Water means birth,' she repeated firmly. 'I bet your mam gets pregnant.'

I knew she was wrong, I was the last my mother would ever have, she told me often enough. But Nancy would not be put off. The book was lacking on nuns, so she held out for the water and maintained that the big empty space was my future.

'There's nothing down for you unless you go with the sisters,' she said.

It was not because I lacked faith that I dreaded the vocation. I suffered from its excesses; it hung around me, watching every move, and passing judgement. I was a failed miserable sinner and I knew it, but I did not want to atone. I did not want the empty future I was sure it offered. Our interpretation of the dream differed.

Around this time I had a Saturday job in a delicatessen in town. I was on the cold-meat counter. None of the girls were allowed to touch the bacon slicer. Only Mr Calderbraith could do that. He wore a white coat and must have fancied himself as an engineer the way he carried on about the gauge of the blades. He would spend hours unscrewing the metal plates and cleaning out the bolts and screws with a look of extreme concentration upon his face.

His balding head put out a few strands of hair which he grew to a ludicrous length and wore combined across his scalp to give the impression of growth. Some of the girls said he wore a toupee after work, and that if we were to meet him on a Sunday, we would not know him.

He used to pretend he was the manager. He would come over and ask customers solicitously if everything was all right and remark that if the service was slow, it was because he was breaking in new staff.

'Who does he think he's kidding!' Elsie said after he had leaned across the counter one morning. 'He couldn't break in his shoes.'

Shoes were a problem. I was on my feet all day, and they would ache by the time we came to cash up. I used to catch the bus from the Pier Head at around five-thirty, if I could get the glass of the counter wiped down and the till cashed. The managers and seniors were obsessed with dishonesty. Cashing-up had to be done in strict military formation. None of us were allowed to move until we heard a bell and the assistant manager would take the cash floats from us in silence.

Inside his glass office the manager sat on a high stool with mirrors all around him, surveying us. If any of the girls sneezed, or moved out of synch, another bell would sound and we would all have to instantly shut our tills while the manager shouted over the loudspeaker system, 'Disturbance at counter number four,' or wherever it was. Sometimes it took ages.

They never failed to inform us that staff were all dishonest. Not the manager, Calderbraith nor the senior staff, but the floor workers, and especially the temporary staff, the Saturday workers, because as they told us, we had the least to lose, and we were 'fly by nights' according to the manager, who grinned as he told us that.

shoulder. Inhuman, they cheeped and shrieked. I could not understand a thing. Mr Calderbraith was nodding at me, his head pecked up and down. I reached out and pointed and a dreadful magnetic force pulled me towards them. I was on my feet in seconds.

Mr Calderbraith turned round and saw the three. He shrank away from them.

'You don't mean these, surely?' he said. 'That is stretching it. Have you been drinking? Tell me, were you on relief at the spirit counter?'

'She's had a bit of a fall,' a passer-by said.

'I think she fell on her head,' Mr Calderbraith nodded.

Then turning to the spectators who had crossed from the bus shelter, he reassured them that everything was all right.

'She is one of my staff members, it's all under control, I know this young lady. Let me deal with it.'

The smallest nun, a tiny frail sparrow, hopped lightly towards me, concern marked by the way she held her head on one side. Her scrawny hand scratched at the ground and she caught up a carrier bag that lay askew on the grass verge. The others clucked solicitously. Then there was a stillness. All fluttering seemed to stop. She handed the bag to me and I took it as my voice returned to tumble out in hopeless apologies while my face burned. Hugging the carrier bag to me, I stumbled towards a taxi which pulled up. I fell inside and slammed the door. I breathed deeply, thinking that I was going to cry from embarrassment. Out of the back window I could see the nuns standing with Mr Calderbraith who was looking about as if he had lost something.

'Where to, love?' the driver asked.

My voice was thin and wavery as I told him. I put my head back and sighed. Only when we were half-way along the Dock Road did I realise that I was still hugging the bag. I peered inside. It was stuffed with pieces of meat, slivers of pork and the ends of joints, all wrapped up in Mr Calderbraith's sandwich papers. There was a great big knuckle of honey roast ham. It would be a sin to waste it.

Then I started to laugh. I couldn't stop. Tears ran down my face. Sister Mercy had told us that we had to be spotless, our souls bleached in God's grace. We had to repent our past and ask Him to take up residence in our hearts. I put my hand into the bag and drew out a piece of meat. I crammed it into my mouth. I swallowed my guilt, ate it whole and let it fill my body. As I chewed I wondered at how I still felt the same. I was no different, only I had become the receiver of stolen goods. I wondered if Mr Calderbraith would be nicer to me? I would not be surprised if he let me have a go on the bacon slicer next weekend.

'Are you all right, love?' the driver asked.

I was choking on a piece of meat.

'I'm fine,' I coughed, scarcely waiting long enough before I stuffed another bit into my mouth. I ate with frenzied gulping sounds. When I looked up I saw the driver watching me in his mirror.

'God but you must be starving,' he said.

I nodded.

'Well, you're a growing girl. You don't know how lucky you are to have all your life in front of you.'

'I do, I really do,' I told him as I pulled another bit of meat off a bone with my teeth. Between mouthfuls I laughed. My one regret was that it wasn't a Friday – I could have doubled my sin without any effort. Then I realised that I had subverted three nuns into being accomplices. What more did I need?

I slapped my knees and howled. God would have to be desperate to want me now.

As the taxi pulled up outside the house I saw the curtains twitch. I did not know how I was going to explain losing my shoe, but nothing could lower my spirits, not even hiccups.

Newgrange, near Drogheda

Feet

SEAMUS DEANE 1988

The important events of birth and death are not neatly tidied away in Irish culture. They are far too significant for that. Usually death is accompanied by the ritual of 'the wake', when family and friends come to pay their last respects to the deceased and to join in sharing the grief; sometimes, also, memories of the dead person's life are shared and celebrated with music and dancing. There is a sense of continuity and mutual support among the living community. But in this sad tale, a young boy has to face his first encounter with death on his own.

The plastic table-cloth hung so far down that I could see only their feet. But I could hear the noise and some of the talk, although I was so crunched up inside that I could make out very little of what they were saying. Besides, Smoky was whimpering as he cuddled up on my stomach and I could feel his body quivering every so often under his fur; every quiver made me deaf to their words and alert to their noise.

He had found me under the table when the room filled with feet, standing at all angles, and he sloped through them and came to huddle himself on me. He felt the dread too. She was going to die after they took her to the hospital. I could hear the clumping of the feet of the ambulance men as they tried to manoeuvre her on a stretcher down the stairs. They would have to lift it high over the banister; the turn was too narrow. The stretcher had red handles. I had seen them when the shiny shoes of the ambulance men appeared in the centre of the room. One had been holding it, folded up, perpendicular, with the handles on the ground beside his shiny black shoes which had a tiny redness in one toe-cap when he put the stretcher handles on to the linoleum. The lino itself was so shiny that there was a redness in it too, at an angle, buried in it like a warmth just under the surface. Una was so hot this morning that, pale and sweaty as she was, she made me think of redness too. It came off her, like heat from a griddle. Her eyes shone with pain and pressure, inflated from the inside.

This was a new illness. I loved the names of the others – diphtheria, scarlet fever or scarletina, rubella, polio, influenza; they almost always ended in an 'o' or an 'a' and made me think of Italian football-players or racing drivers or chess-players. Besides, each had its own smell, especially diphtheria, because of the disinfected sheets that were hung over the bedroom doors and billowed out their acrid fragrances in the draughts that chilled your ankles on the stairs. Even the mumps, which came after the diphtheria, was a sickness that did not frighten, because the word was as funny as the shape of everybody's face, all swollen, as if there had been a terrific fight. But this was a new sickness. This was called meningitis. It was a word you had to bite on to say it. It had a fright and a hiss in it. It didn't make me think of anything except Una's eyes widening all the time and getting lighter, as if helium were pumping into them from her brain. They would burst, I thought, unless they could find a way of getting all that pure helium pain out. I wondered if they could.

They were at the bottom of the stairs. All the feet moved that way. I could see Uncle Manus's brown shoes; the heels were worn down, and he was hesitating, moving back and forward a little. Uncle Dan and Uncle Tom had identical shoes, heavy and rimed with mud and cement, because they had come from the building site in Creggan. Dan's were dirtier, though, because Tom was the foreman. But they weren't good shoes. Dan put one knee up on a chair and I squirmed flat to see the scabs on the sole of the one that was in mid-air. There was putlock oil on his socks and black bars of it on the sole. But it was my mother's and father's feet that I watched most. She was wearing low heels that badly needed mending, and her feet were always swollen so that, even from there, I could see the shoe leather embedded, vanishing into her ankles.

There was more scuffle and noise and her feet disappeared into the hallway, after the stretcher, and she was cough-crying as my father's work-boots followed close behind her, huge, with the laces thonged round the back. Then everybody went out and the room was empty.

Smoky shook under his fur. It was cold in there with all the doors open and the winter air darkening. She was going to die and she was younger than me. She was only six. I tried to imagine her not there. She would go to heaven, for sure. Wouldn't she miss us? What could you do in heaven, except smile? All the same, she had a great smile.

Everybody came in again. There wasn't much talking. My father stood near the table. I could smell the quays off his dungarees, the aroma of horizons where ships grew to a speck and disappeared. Every day he went to work I felt he was going out foreign, as we said; and every day when he came back, I was relieved that he had changed his mind. Tom was pushing a spirit-level into a long leg-pocket of his American boiler suit, and Dan picked up his coat, which had fallen off a chair on to the floor. I could see the dermatitis stains on his fingers and knuckles. He was allergic to the plaster he had to work with every day. Next month, he'd be off work, his hands all scabs and sores. Where would Una be next month?

They all left except my parents. He was at the table again, very close. My mother was standing at the press-cupboard, a couple of feet away, her shoes pressed together, looking very small. She was still crying. My father's boots moved towards her until they were very close. He was saying something. Then he got closer, almost stood on her shoes, which moved apart. One of his boots was between her feet. There was her shoe, then his boot, then her shoe, then his boot. I looked at Smoky, who licked my face. He was kissing her. She was still crying. Their feet shifted and I thought she was going to fall for one shoe came off the ground for a second. Then they steadied and they just stood there like that and everything was silent and I scarcely breathed.

That was my first death. When the priest tossed the first three shovelfuls of clay on to the coffin, the clattering sound seemed to ring all over the hillside graveyard and my father's face moved sideways as if he had been struck.

We were all lined up on the lip of the grave which was brown and narrow, so much so that the ropes they had looped through the coffin handles came up stained with the dun earth. One of the grave-diggers draped the ropes over a headstone before he started heaving the great mound of clay on top of her. The clay came up to the brim as though it were going to boil over. We placed flowers and leaned our hands on the cold earth as we had leaned them on the glossy coffin top and as we had pressed them on her waxen hands the night before at the wake, where one candle burned and no drink was taken. When we got back, the candle was out and my mother was being comforted by aunts and neighbours who all wore the same serious and determined expression of compassion and sternness, so that even the handsome and the less-than-handsome all looked alike. The men doffed their caps and looked into the distance. No one looked anyone else in the face, it seemed.

The children appeared here and there, their faces at angles behind or between adults, fascinated, like angels staring into the light. I went up to the bedroom where she had lain and sat on my bed and looked at hers and buried my face in the pillow where her pain had been, saying her name inside my head but not out loud, breathing for something of her but only finding the scent of cotton, soap, of a life rinsed out and gone. When I heard noise on the stairs, I came out to see my uncles lifting the third bed from that downstairs room up over the banisters. They told me to stand aside as they worked it into the room and put the bed where she was waked beside the bed where she had been sick. The wake bed was a better one, with a headboard. Deirdre or Eilis would have a bed to herself.

Una came back only once, some weeks later. My mother had asked me to visit the grave and put flowers on it. They would have to be wild flowers, since shop flowers were too expensive. I forgot until it was almost four o'clock and getting dark. I ran to the graveyard, hoping it would not be shut. But it was too late. The gates were padlocked. I cut up the lane alongside the east wall until I reached the corner where the wall had collapsed about two feet from the top. It was easy to climb over and inside there was an untended area where the grass was long and where I had seen flowers growing before. But there were none, not even on the stunted hedgerow beneath the wall – not a berry, not a husk. I pulled some long grass and tried to plait it, but it was too wet and slippery. I threw the long stems away into the mottled air and they fell apart as they disappeared.

Running between the little pathways which separated the graves, I got lost several times before I found the fresh grave and recognised the withered flowers as those we had left a short time before. I pulled the wreaths apart, hoping to find some flowers not so badly withered, but there were very few. A torn rose, a chrysanthemum as tightly closed as a nut, some irises that were merely damp stalks with a tinge of blue – that was all. But I couldn't get them to hold together with the bits of wire from the original wreaths, so I scooped at the ground and put them in a bunch together, pressing the earth round them with my foot. All the while, I was saying her name over and over. Una, Una, Una, Una, Una. It was dark and I felt contrite and lonely, fearful as well. 'I have to go,' I said to the ground, 'I have to go. I don't like leaving you, but I have to go, Una.' The wall seemed far away. I got up off my knees and rubbed my hands on my socks. 'I'll come back soon. 'Bye.'

I set off at a run, along the dark pathways, zig-zagging round headstones and great glass bells in which flowers were stifling, Celtic crosses, raised statues, lonely, bare plots, a fresh grave where the flowers still had some colour even in the light that the trees were swallowing into their trunks and branches. She came right down the path before me for an instant, dressed in her usual tartan skirt and jumper, her hair tied in ribbons, her smile sweeter than ever. Even as I said her name she wasn't there and I was running on, saying her name again, frightened now, until I reached the wall and looked back from the broken top stones over the gloomy hillside and its heavy burden of dead. Then I ran again until I reached the street-lamps on the Lone Moor Road, and scraped the mud off my shoes against the kerb and brushed what I could of it from my clothes. I walked home, slowly. I was late but being a bit later did not matter now. I didn't know if I would tell or not; that depended on what I was asked. I knew it would upset my mother, but, then again, it might console her to think Una was still about, although I wished she wasn't wandering about that graveyard on her own.

My older brother, Liam, settled the issue for me. I met him in the street and told him instantly. At first he was amused, but then got angry when I wondered aloud if I should tell my mother. 'Are you out of your head, or what? You'd drive her mad; she's out of her mind anyway sending you for flowers this time o' year. Sure any half-sane person would have said Yes and done nothing. Anyway, you saw nothing. You say nothing. You're not safe to leave alone.'

All night I lay thinking of her and hearing again the long wail of agony from my mother half-way through the family rosary. It made everybody stand up and Smoky crawled back under the table. I wished I could go in there with him but we all just stood there as she cried and pulled her hair and almost fought my father's consoling arms away. All her features were so stretched I hardly recognised her. It was like standing in the wind at night, listening to her. She cried all night. Every so often I would hear her wail, so desolate it seemed distant, and I thought of Una in the graveyard, standing under all those towering stone crosses, her ribbons red.

The Year 1912

MÁIRTÍN Ó CADHAIN 1948

Ireland has been a restless country for centuries, with invaders and religious and political troubles. For over 200 years, young people have been emigrating in search of prosperity, trying to find work and to earn money to send back to their families. Nowadays, millions of people can call themselves Irish, in the USA, Canada, Britain and elsewhere; but most of these are to be found in the USA, which was always their main goal. The farewell party for a person emigrating is known as an 'American Wake'. This story shows the hope and excitement and the grief that such partings can bring.

'The trunk.'

She said the word offhand yet there was a touch of stubbornness in her tone. She hadn't agreed to go to Brightcity with her daughter a week ago last Saturday to buy the trunk, and it irked her like a white frost the way it had been perched up on the ledge of the kitchen dresser, adored like an idol. The children having great play with it, opening it, closing it, looking it all over. She hadn't the heart to vex her daughter this final week, otherwise she would have cleared it off into the room under the bed. But tonight, though the daughter might be of a different mind and anxious to show off that expensive article to the company that had gathered, the mother had followed her own inclination at nightfall and moved the trunk into the room – it might, she said, get damaged or scratched where it was.

It was like a burnt spot or a smallpox scar on the face of life, tonight especially since she seldom had a hearty gathering under her roof. It was useful and wellmade, but that was only a chimaera, a ghost from the Otherworld come to snatch away the first conception of her womb and the spring of her daily life, just when the drinking, the high spirits, the music and merrymaking were in full spate. Seven weeks ago, before the passage-money came, she had been as much on edge awaiting it as Mairin was. That her daughter should be off to America was no surprise to her, no more than the eight sisters of her own whose going was a bitter memory still. She had been schooled by the iron necessities of life to keep a grip on her feelings and throttle her motherlove – as Eve ought to have throttled the serpent of Knowledge. It was the passage-money that had set the heather ablaze again. Flickers of affection, flashes of insight from shut-away feelings, were setting her sense and reason aglow with the knowledge that this going into exile was worse than the spoiling of a church or the wreck of a countryside . . . .

But it was destiny, must be attended to. The day was agreed. Patch Thomais was gone for the sidecar. Back in the crowded kitchen the merriment had risen to a frenzy; remnants of the wreck of a people, doomed to extinction at daybreak, bringing their ritual vigil to a hurried night's-end climax of wild debauch . . . .

A halfpenny candle stood on a small press by the wall in the bedroom, smeared by a breeze coming by the edge of the paper on a broken windowpane. Depth, magic, mystery of unfathomable seas, reflected by the guttering candleflame in the trunk's brass knobs. It was of pale yellow timber, the mother couldn't at once remember where she had seen that colour before – the face of a corpse after a long wake in sultry weather. And a certain distaste kept her from looking into the trunk, that same tabu which had kept her, though she had often tried, from looking at a corpse in a coffin.

'Have you everything?' she asked the daughter keeping her eyes off the dimlit thing. There were all kinds of things in it – a sod of turf, a chip off the hearthstone, tresses of hair, a bunch of shamrock though it was autumn, stockings of homespun, a handful of dulse, items of clothing, papers connected with the voyage across. The daughter took her shoes, coat, hat and dress out of the trunk and laid them on the little press to put on her. During the week she had often laid them out like that but the mother had never encouraged her, and early in the night she had implored her not to put them on till morning.

The mother shut the trunk, threw the bedquilt over it. 'To keep it clean.' She had long feared that the daughter once she was in the American clothes would be estranged from her, alien as the trunk. Mairin was in her stocking feet and naked except for a long white shift which she had been at great pains to fix about herself that evening and which she had no intention of taking off until she had reached the house of a relative on the other side. Seeing her like that was to see a vision, the only one which had remained clearskinned and beautiful in her memory. A vision that gave bodily shape to the dear lost Tree of Life, while it made real the delicate and deceitful skin of the Knowledge -Apple – a mother's first conception, first fruit. She had so many things on the tip of her tongue to say to her, the intimacies, the affectionate things saved up in motherlove, her life-stuff, from the moment she feels the quick seed in her womb until the flush of eternity puts out the twilight of the world.

For a month now she had said many things to the daughter, scraps scattered at long intervals . . . that she couldn't care if all in the house were to go so long as Mairin stayed . . . that the whole house would miss her, herself especially . . . that of all her children she was the one who had given her the least trouble . . . that she was fine about a house. But none of all that said what she wanted to say. She felt like a serving-woman, the necklace she was putting about the young queen's neck had broken, its precious stones scattered here and there in danger of being crushed and broken. She felt as if some hostile force were filtering her speech, hindering her from letting loose the flow of talk that would ease the tight grip on her heart. She was aware she could never hope to express the things in her mind in a letter which she would have to depend on someone else to write, and in a language whose make and meaning were as unhomely to her as the make and meaning of the Ghost from the Fairymound. And a letter was a poor substitute for the living contact of speech, eyes, features. Her flowing imagination, floodtide of her love, would run thin and freeze in a niggardly writing.

She was hardly likely to see her daughter again for a very long time. Mairin would have to repay her passage, then earn the passage of one or two more of the family, as well as send a share home. It could happen that the child in her womb would set eyes on her before she did. That American coat, the graveclothes – how tell one from the other? The 'God speed her' that would be said from now on had for its undermeaning 'God have mercy on her soul.' Children often got those two expressions mixed up. And when the time came that in actual fact would change the 'God speed' into 'God have mercy,' it would come without a decent laying-out and a bier to be carried, and with no passionate keen. Even the graveclothes, no mother would have them awhile to shake out the folds of them from time to time as a relief to her anguish, and there would be neither name nor surname on a rough bit of board in the churchyard by the Fiord for generations to come. The voyage – that immensity, cold and sterile – would erase the name from the genealogy of the race. She would go as the wild geese go.

But while such ideas were as a sour curd in the mother's mind, she wouldn't give in to the thought that she would never see the daughter again. Her sense and reason said no, her love, hope, determination said yes. And it was these she listened to. Yet even if she were to see her again she knew she'd be utterly unlike the simple country girl, now nineteen years old, with a look pure as morningsun on a hillside in the Promised Land. Her lips would have been embittered by the berries from the Tree of Good and Evil. That dark weasel envy in her heart. Experience, that slimy serpent, writhing in her mind. Temper of cold steel in her countenance. The tone of her voice transformed by the spell of a harsh stepmother. Such were all returned Americans. She must reveal herself to her now, as the mother of the warriors in the cave used to reveal herself to her children when every sallying out in search of food was a matter of life and death. Reveal herself to her while her age and ignorance were still unmocked at, while there was yet no wall of disbelief between her daughter's mind and hers . . . .

The money, she thought, was the best way to begin. She took a cloth purse from her bosom, took out what small change the daughter might need in Brightcity, and gave her the purse with the rest. The daughter hung it about her neck and settled it carefully in her breast under her holy scapular.

'Look now, child, you take good care of it. It's likely you won't need it at all, but if you fail to find work soon it would be too much to be depending on Aunt Nora who has her own children to look after. Keep the rug tucked well round you on the vessel. Make free with no one unless it happens to be someone you know. You'll be safe as soon as you reach Nora's house. Even if you have to take small pay, don't overstrain yourself working . . . . You will make a visit home after five years. Well, at least after ten years . . . . It can't be but you'll have a few pence put by by then. My . . . .'

She had kept her spirits nicely up to that. But as soon as she thought to break the crust of speech she couldn't find a word to say but stood stockstill staring at her daughter. Hands fiddling with the folds of her apron. Blushing, tears and smiles painfully together in her cheek. Humps and wrinkles of distress coming in her forehead like keys struggling with a lock. The daughter was almost dressed by now and asked where was the small change she'd need in Brightcity? The mother had been so eager to talk that she had forgotten to get a little purse to put it in. Turning to get it she fell into such confusion she forgot the money in her fist until it fell and scattered about the floor. Her idea had been to wait till her tongue could contrive a proper speech, then to hand over the small change to the daughter as a sacred offering, embrace and kiss her . . . . Instead, the sacrifice had been ripped from her hand.

Putting away the little purse the daughter felt an envelope in her pocket.

'A tress of your hair, mama,' she said. 'I thought I had put it in the trunk alongwith – the rest.' She held the black tress between her and the candle, her blue eyes softened, became childlike. She felt an urge to say something to her mother, she didn't quite know what. Her thoughts went fumbling here and there as a stranger might among the blind holes of a bog on a dark night. The pair of them would have to be in the one bed, the light out, and a wand of moonlight through the small window to charm and set free the tongue. She looked her mother in the eyes to see if she might find encouragement there, but she remained unconscious of her mother's seething emotions, locked within, quite unable to crack the fixed and rigid mask of her features.

She put on the light and gaudy coat, then the wide-brimmed hat. Part of the preparations for her attack on life, she supposed, was to spend a long time fixing and refixing the set of the hat, though she had no idea which particular slant she wanted. She didn't realise that the size and the undulations of the hatbrim added nothing to her good looks, nor that the yellow shoes, black hat and red coat made a devil's own trinity in conflict with her fresh and delicate features. But she was ready: hat, coat, low shoes on and lady-gloves – not to be taken off again. She felt strange, surprised as a butterfly that feels for the first time that it has shed its cramped caterpillar limbs and has the endless airy spaces unimpeded to sail through on easy wings. She felt too some of the light-headed pride of the butterfly . . . .

The mother forgot until the trunk had been locked that she had forgotten to put a bit of hendirt in it, or somewhere among the daughter's clothing. But she wouldn't for the world unlock it again. She couldn't bear the daughter to make fun of her, this morning especially, accuse her of pishrogues and superstition. She shook a tint of holy water on her, and while she was putting the feather back in the bottle the daughter was off out to the kitchen floor to show off her American ensemble.

The sidecar hadn't come yet. There was a swirl of dancing. Tom Neile with his back to the closed door was singing *The Three Sons* in a drunken voice drowning the music –

There's many a fine spa-a-rk young and hea-a-rty
Went over the wa-a-ter and ne-e-e-r return'd.

'Tone yourself down,' said the mother to Tom, but she'd have given a deal just then to have a tune like he had in order to release the load of her love in a spilling song. The girls had gathered again about the daughter, scrutinising her rig-out, although they had been a week looking at it. They gave the mother no chance of keeping her company. They thought nothing, it seemed to her, of driving a wedge into nature, one almost as inhuman as that driven in by the immense cold sterile sea. The young women were chirruping of America. Chirruping of the life they'd have together soon in South Boston. Typical of a race whose guardian angel was the American trunk, whose guiding star was the exile ship, whose Red Sea was the Atlantic. Bidin Johnny reminded her to ask her cousin to hurry with the passage-money. Judeen Sheain told her on her life not to forget to tell Liam Pheige about the fun there was at the wake of old Cait Thaidhg.

'Take care you don't forget to tell our Sean that we have the Mountain Garth under potatoes again this year,' said Sorcha Phaidin. He said when he was going that after him no one would ever again be born to the race that would attempt to sow it, it was such a hardship.

'Tell my boy, Mairin, that it won't be long till I'll be over to him,' Nora Phadraig Mhurcha said in a whisper that all the girls heard.

'By cripes it won't be long till I'm knocking sparks out of the paving stones of South Boston myself,' said a redhead youth whose tongue had been loosed by the drink.

'God help those that have to stay at home,' said old Seamas Ó Currain.

The whiskey was circling again. 'Here now, you ought to take a taste of it,' said Peaitsin Shiubhaine who was measuring it out, heeling the glass towards Mairin with a trembling hand. He splashed some of it on her coat. 'A mouthful of it will do you no harm. Devil the drop of poteen you're likely to see for the rest of your life.' There was an undertone to his voice, he was remembering the five daughters of his own who were 'beyond' – one of them thirty-five years gone – and he had no hope of ever seeing them again . . . . 'I'll drink it myself then. Your health, Mairin, and God bring you safe to journey's end.'

Neither Peaitsin nor anyone else in the gathering thought to add, 'God send you safe home again.' Such ignorance of the proper thing to say sparked off the mother's repressed anger. 'Five years from today you'll see her back home again,' she said tartly.

'God grant it,' said Peaitsin and Seainin Thomais Choilm together.

'And she'll marry a monied man and stay here with us for good,' laughed Citin, Mairin's aunt.

'I'll have little or nothing to show after five years,' said Mairin. 'But maybe you'd marry me youself, Seainin, without a sixpence?'

But by this time Seainin had huddled himself back against the door and was talking like a tornado to let the mockery of the young girls pass over him.

'At all costs don't pick up an accent,' said a young lad, one of her cousins, 'and don't be "guessing" all round you like Micilin Eamoinn who spent only two months beyond and came home across the fields with nothing to show for his voyage but half a guinea and a new waistcoat.'

'Nor asking "What's that, mamma?" when you see the pig.'

'Anyhow, you'll send me my passage,' said Mairead the next daughter to Mairin, eyes sparkling.

'And mine too,' said Norin the next sister.

The mother felt a bleak touch of her own death hearing the greedy begging voices of the pair. Years of delay were being heaped on her daughter's return, as shovelfuls of earth are heaped on a coffin. And the grace of that home-coming was receding from her – as far as Judgement Day. At that moment the children she had given birth to were her greatest enemies.

She set Mairin to drink tea again though she had just stood up from it. But she wanted to come close to her again. She must break bread, make a farewell communion, weave the intimate bond of a farewell supper with her daughter. She would tell her plain and straight that she didn't believe this parting meal to be a funeral meal as far as home was concerned: there would be an Easter to come, before the Judgement. But they weren't left to themselves. Her sister Citin with her family of daughters and some of the other girls pushed up to the table by the wall and in no time had Mairin engulfed among them.

The daughter had no wish for food. Her face burned: desire, panic, wonder, an anguish of mind, all showed in her cheek. Brightcity was the farthest from home she had ever been, but she had been nurtured on American lore from infancy. South Boston, Norwood, Butte, Montana, Minnesota, California, plucked chords in her imagination more distinctly than did Dublin, Belfast, Wexford, or even places only a few miles out on the Plain beyond Brightcity. Life and her ideas of it had been shaped and defined by the fame of America, the wealth of America, the amusements of America, the agonised longing to go to America . . . . And though she was lonesome now at leaving home it was a lonesomeness shot through and through with hope, delight, wonder. At last she was on the threshold of the Fairy Palace . . . . Tremendous seas, masts and yardarms, blazing lights, silvertoned streets, dark people whose skin gleamed like beetles, distorting for her already the outlines of garth, mountain, rock, fiord. Her mind tonight was nothing but a ragbag to keep the castoff shreds of memory in until she might shed them as flotsam as she sailed. She was so unguarded now that she let herself be led out to dance on the stone floor, dressed as she was for America. In any case she couldn't have found it in her heart to refuse Padraigin Phaidin.

It irked her conscience that she had so long neglected him. She began to dance in a lackadaisical way, but the pulse of the music – that music to which they were beholden even in the fairyplace – excited an impulse in herself, and soon in her dappled outfit she was like a young alien deer, fullblooded, with the common young animals of the herd prancing about her, inciting her to show what she was made of, what she could do, while the elders sat around in sage contemplation. The mother was thinking that if she was ever to see her again the hard experience of life would then be a dead weight on that lust for dancing. In place of that passion of young and eager blood that wedded her limbs to the graceful movement of the stars, the thin and watery stuff of greying age would be keeping her tired bones fixed on earth.

Nevertheless the mother was closely watching, not the daughter, but Padraigin Phaidin who was dancing with her. There and then she guessed the whole story. Easy to see. Very likely the pair had never said a word of love to each other. Very likely they hadn't said a word tonight. And they were likely never to say a word in their lives. But she realised they would be married in South Boston in a year's time, in five years, ten years even . . . . She was vexed. That's what lay behind Padraigin's wild dancing fit. What she had failed to say in words he was saying in dance. Body and limbs he was enacting a perfect poem, with growing zest, abandon, vigour and precision, until a lash of his nailed boot carved a spark out of the hearthstone in time with the final beat of the music. Some might put it down to intoxication, but the mother knew better. That spark was in fact a finishing touch, a final fling of the spirit in full victory. Then hardly waiting to be asked while still breathless from the dance he began with easy power to sing. And the mother forgot the daughter listening to him:

The garden's a desert, dear heart, and lonesome I be,
No fruit on the bough, no flower on the thorn, no leaf,
No harping is heard and no bird sings in the tree
Since the love of my heart, white branch, went to Cashel O'Neill.

A young spirit trying to crack the shell of a universe that shut it in, so fierce was his song. By now the mother had come to hate him. An evil being, fingering her own proper treasure . . . .

Horse's hooves and the clatter of a sidecar were heard from the cart-track outside. Music and merriment ceased suddenly. Only Seainin Tolan stretched drunk against the shut door still moaning –

Ora, wora, wora,
It's on the southern side of New York quay
That I myself will land –

the only snatch of a song Seainin ever raised.

'Indeed you'd be a nice gift to America! Devil drown and extinguish you, it's a pity it isn't on some quay you are, a useless hulk, instead of here,' cried a youth who could stand him no longer.

The trunk was taken from the room and set like a golden calf on the table.

'Take out that and tie it up on the sidecar,' said the mother.

'It might get broken,' said Mairin. 'Leave it alone until I'm ready to go out along with it.' That trunk was her licence and authority to wear an elegant hat on her head and an ostentatious coat on her back instead of a shawl. Without the trunk her lady-outfit would be an insult to God. If she let it out of her sight for as much as a second as like as not those tricksome and showy garments would wither into rags and ashes about her body.

She turned now to say goodbye to those who hadn't the strength to accompany her as far as the king's highway. Crippled oldtimers who could barely manage to shuffle across the street; for most of them this was likely the last time they'd leave their own firesides for a social occasion. This was the first link of the chain to be jerked apart, it made her feel for the first time how hard the parting was, how merciless. Whatever about the rest of the people, she would never set eyes on these again. In spite of her distress and hurry she looked closely at each one of them so as to store up in her memory their shape and features. She kept a grip on her emotion and broke down only when she came to her grandmother at the hearth. She had as much affection for her grandmother as she had for her mother, and made more free with her. And was loved in return. Never a week went by but the old woman had laid aside a bit of her pension to give her, whatever else might be behindhand. The old creature was as speechless as if already turned to clay. In fact she almost was, for the best part of her was in the grip of 'the One with the thin hard foot,' and the rest waiting on busy death to prepare her dwelling-place. Her mouth was as dry as the timber of a new-shut coffin, and except for a faint blinking of the eyelids that brought her far-off look a little closer to the here and now, Mairin would have thought that she hadn't the least notion what was going on.

'I'll never see you again, mammo,' she said, her voice breaking at last in tears.

'God is good,' said the mother, a shade stubborn.

Then to kiss the small children and the infant in the cradle. She felt it as a warm substantial summer after the midwinter chill. Charming her senses against the threat of the graveclothes.

The mother brought her off to the room once more. But they weren't long there till Citin and Mairead came in on them to get their shawls so as to accompany Mairin to Brightcity. The mother could have melted them. How officious they were – without them, she thought, the lump of sorrow in her throat wouldn't have hardened again. All she could say to Mairin was that she'd have good earnings; that she hoped they'd have good weather at sea; and for the life of her not to forget to have her picture taken beyond and send it home.

'My own darling girl,' she said, picking a speck of fluff from the shoulder of the coat and giving a hurried quirk to the hatbrim, though the daughter at once reset it her own way. And having glanced quickly round the house she was ready to go.

The sidecar went lurching down the rugged village track followed by a dense crowd, men, women and children. They had all the appearance of a sacrificial procession: the sidecar like a funeral pyre ahead, puffs of the men's tobacco-smoke hanging in the early morning air, and Mairin walking in her barbaric costume as the officiating druid.

The mother walked alongside the daughter and offered to carry her rug, but Brid Sheamais snatched it and carried it herself. She had determined to have Mairin under her own wing on this last walk, but Citin and her own Mairead thwarted her once more. Then all the young girls closed round her, some chattering and laughing, some so lonesome at her going that they hadn't the heart to say much, and others sorry that they weren't in her place or going along with her. By this time the mother had hardly any feelings of regret left so angry was she with the rabble that wished to deprive her of her daughter before she was even out of sight. She took a spleen against the sidecar too. It was moving as fast as if it was giving a corpse 'the quick trot to the graveyard'. It seemed to her that it was the trunk – perked up on the box of the car, its timber blond as an ear of corn in the rays of the virgin sun – that was pricking the horse to death's own scything speed. She hadn't a word left to say . . . .

There was a mild red light from the sun just up. Field walls and piles of stone grinned bleakly. In the little pokes of fields slanting and rugged the tramped stubble was like the head of some Samson having suffered the shears of Delilah. A small sailingboat just out from harbour with a fair wind scratched a bright wake down the Fiord. Mairin looked back from the rise at Hollycliff, from then on her own house and the village houses strung around would be out of sight. Last year's new thatch joined the old black and withered roof at the ridge-strip – line of contact between the past and the time to come. And the village seemed asleep again after its brief second of action, slight as a spit in the ocean that the sailingboat might obliterate.

The sidecar halted at the end of the track. The people formed a close group in the mouth of the highway so that the mother was cut off from the daughter. Just another stray stone in the cairn, that's all she was. The same as if she was neither kith nor kin. More than ever she begrudged Citin and Mairead their going to Brightcity with Mairin. When the kissing began the women were like a gaggle of scavengers about a prey. They pushed their way rudely up to her daughter, squeezed her hand, snatched kisses one after the other like a flock of starlings on a trash-heap. The men shook hands with her, shy, laconic, seeming to say it was all one, and if it had to be done then it were best done as quickly as might be. Padraigin Phaidin did likewise, but unlike the rest of the men he gave the slightest lift to his head and the mother caught the eyes of the couple interlocked for the nick of a second.

At last it was her turn. She hadn't kissed her daughter since she was a child. But she failed to put much yearning and anguish into the kiss, though her lips hungered for her. Hadn't she kissed all and everyone? Hadn't all and everyone got ahead of herself in the kissing and hugging? The daughter's kiss was cold and insipid, the good skimmed from it by all that had been pecking at her. Her body was cold too, cold and insubstantial as a changeling from the Liss.

But what quite spoiled the kiss for her was the sight of the trunk, she was unable to keep her eyes off it and it was all but whispering in her ear –

No mortal kiss will break the spell of the changeling, seduced by pleasure to wander and forget, whose dwelling is the golden web which young desires weave from the sunlight on green hills far off from the here and now.

Mairin was now on the sidecar. Mairead sitting beside her, Citin next to the driver on the other side, Padraigin Phaidin fixing the trunk firmly between them up on the box. Damned spirits, they appeared to the mother – the accursed trunk, Mairead greedy to get her passage-money, and Padraigin Phaidin on edge to get to America and marry her daughter – three damned spirits torturing her first-born and best-beloved.

Padraigin had finished and the people were moving aside to make way for the horse. The women started in to sob, and the sobbing lifted into a loud wail of words, expressing no real anguish the mother thought, beyond voice and tears. They wouldn't leave her even the comfort of keening alone. And she shed no tear . . . .

She stammered uncertainly, 'I'll see you before five years are out.' And couldn't raise her eyes to meet the eyes of her daughter, not if the sky fell.

The car was now moving. Sobbing, the daughter whimpered, 'You will.' But now the mother's heart as well as her common sense knew that she would not. Padraigin Phaidin would see her sooner and the girls of the village and her own children, even the infant then in her womb. The mother realised she was but the first of the nestlings in flight to the land of summer and joy: the wild goose that would never again come back to its native ledge.

An Irish Island by Dermot McCarthy

Village Without Men

MARGARET BARRINGTON 1982

Life in the tiny islands of the west has always been a harsh and unforgiving matter. From the time of the early Celts, and then the invading Danes, the population lived off the land and the rich but treacherous sea. When the sea's storms devour their men, the widowed women of this story cling to their island lives with a ferocious courage until, one day, they are rewarded as history and folk-tale become an exciting reality.

Weary and distraught the women listened to the storm as it raged around the houses. The wind screamed and howled. It drove suddenly against the doors with heavy lurchings. It tore at the straw ropes which anchored the thatched roofs to the ground. It rattled and shook the small windows. It sent the rain in narrow streams under the door, through the piled-up sacks, to form large puddles on the hard stamped earthen floors.

At times when the wind dropped for a moment to a low whistling whisper and nothing could be heard but the hammering of the sea against the face of Cahir Roe, the sudden release would be intolerable. Then one or another would raise her head and break into a prayer, stumbling words of supplication without continuity or meaning. Just for a moment a voice would be heard. Then the screaming wind would rise again in fury, roaring in the chimney and straining the roof-ropes, the voice would sink to a murmur and then to nothing as the women crouched again over the smouldering sods, never believing for a moment in the miracle they prayed for.

Dawn broke and the wind dropped for a while. The women wrapped their shawls tightly round them, knotted the ends behind them and tightened their headcloths. They slipped out through cautiously opened doors. The wind whipped their wide skirts so tightly to their bodies it was hard to move. They muttered to themselves as they clambered over the rocks or waded through the pools down to the foaming sea.

To the right Cahir Roe sloped upward, smothered in storm clouds, protecting the village from the outer sea. The ears of the women rang with the thunder of the ocean against its giant face. Salt foam flecked their faces, their clothes as they struggled along in knots of three or four, their heads turned from the wind as they searched the shore and looked out over the rolling water. But in all that grey-green expanse of churning sea, nothing. Not even an oar. All day long they wandered.

It was not until the turn of the tide on the second day that the bodies began to roll in, one now, another again, over and over in the water like dark, heavy logs. Now a face showed, now an outstretched hand rose clear of the water. John Boyle's face had been smashed on the rocks, yet his wife knew him as an incoming wave lifted his tall lean body to hurl it to shore.

For two days the women wandered until the ocean, now grown oily but still sullen with anger, gave up no more. Neil Boylan, Charley Friel and Dan Gallagher were never found.

The women rowed across the bay to the little town of Clonmullen for the priest. After the heavy rain the road across the bog was dangerous, and the village was cut off by land. The young curate, Father Twomey, came across. When he looked at the grey haggard faces of these women, all words of comfort deserted the young priest. His throat went dry and his eyes stung as if the salt sea had caught them. What comfort could words bring to women in their plight? He could with greater ease pray for the souls of the drowned than encourage the living to bear their sorrow in patience.

The women had opened the shallow graves in the sandy graveyard. They lowered the bodies and shovelled back the sand. Then for headstones, to mark the place where each man was laid before the restlesss sand should blot out every sign, they drove an oar which he had handled into each man's grave and dropped a stone there for every prayer they said. The wind blew the sand into the priest's vestments, into his shoes, into his well-oiled hair and into his book. It whirled the sand around the little heaps of stones.

As the women rowed him home across the bay, the priest looked back at the village. The oars in the graves stood out against the stormy winter sky like the masts of ships in harbour.

The midwife was the first to leave the village.

As they brought each dead man up from the sea, she stripped him and washed his body. For most of them she had done this first service. From early youth, first with her mother, then alone, she had plied her trade on this desolate spit of land. These same bodies which once warm, soft, tender and full of life, had struggled between her strong hands, now lay cold and rigid beneath them. She washed the cold sea-water from these limbs from which she had once washed the birth-slime. Silently she accomplished her task and retired to her cottage. Of what use was a midwife in a village without men?

She wrote to her married daughter in Letterkenny who replied that there was work in plenty for her there. Then two weeks later when the hard frosts held the bog road, she loaded her goods on a cart and set out for Clonmullen from where she could get the train to Letterkenny. She took with her young Laurence Boyle, John Boyle's 14-year-old son, to bring back the donkey and cart.

The women watched her go. A few called God-speed but the others, thin-lipped, uttered no word. Silently they went back to their houses and their daily tasks. From now on their bodies would be barren as fields in winter.

All winter the village lay dumb and still. The stores of potatoes and salt fish were eaten sparingly. The fish might run in the bay now, followed by the screaming seagulls, but there were no men to put out the boats or draw in the gleaming nets. The children gathered mussels to feed the hens.

Then in the early spring days, the women rose from their hearths, and tightly knotted their headcloths and shawls. They took down the wicker creels from the lofts, the men's knives from the mantleshelves and went down to the rocks below Cahir Roe to cut the sea-wrack for the fields. The children spread it on the earth. Then with fork and spade the women turned the light sandy soil, planted their potatoes, oats and barley. The work was heavy and backbreaking but it had to be done. If they did not work now with all their strength, their children would be crying for food in the coming winter.

Driven, bone-tired, sick at heart, they rose early and worked all day, stopping at midday as their husbands had stopped, to rest in the shelter of a stone wall, to drink some milk or cold tea and to eat some oatbread the children brought to them in the fields. At night they dragged their bodies to bed. There was no joy, no relief to be got there now. Nothing but sleep, easing of weary muscles.

Their work in the house was neglected. The hearths went untended, their clothes unwashed. They no longer white-washed the walls of the cottages or tended the geraniums they grew in pots. They did not notice when the flowers died.

The next to leave the village was Sally Boyle. She was to have married young Dan Gallagher after the next Lent. There at the end of the straggling village was the half-built ruin of the house he had been getting ready with the help of the other men in the village. All winter she moped over the fire, only rousing herself when her mother's voice rose sharp and angry. Now in the spring she began to wander about restlessly. She would leave her work and climb the great headland of Cahir Roe, there to look out to where Tory rose like a fortress from the sea – out there across the sea in which Dan Gallagher had been drowned, the sea which had refused to surrender what should have been hers. At night in bed she could not control the wildness of her body. She pitched from side to side, moaning and muttering. Her whole mind was darkened by the memory of soft kisses on warm autumn nights, of strong hands fondling her. She felt bereft, denied.

She slipped away one day and joined the lads and lasses in Clonmullen who were off to the hiring fair at Strabane. Later her mother got a letter and a postal order for five shillings. Sally was now hired girl on a farm down in the Lagan.

Then in ones and twos the young girls began to leave. With the coming of spring their eyes brightened, their steps grew lighter. They would stop and look over their shoulders hurriedly as if someone were behind. They would rush violently to work and then leave their tasks unfinished to stand and look out over the landscape, or out to sea from under a sheltering hand. They became irritable, quarrelsome and penitent by turns. Somewhere out there across the bog, across the sea, lay a world where men waited; men who could marry them, love them perhaps, give them homes and children.

The women objected to their going and pleaded with them. Every hand was needed now. The turf must be cut in the bog, turned and stacked for the coming winter. Surely they could go when the crops were gathered in. But tears and pleading were in vain. Nature fought against kindness in their young bodies. Here no men were left to promise these girls life, even the hazardous life of this country. They gathered their few garments together and departed, promising to send back what money they could. But their mothers knew that it was not to get money they left. It was the blood in their veins which drove them forth. And though the women lamented, they understood.

No use now to give a dance for the departing girls. There were no men with whom they could dance. No use to gather the neighbours into the house to sing. The voices of women are thin and shrill without men's voices to balance them.

Larry Boyle found himself the only lad in the village. The other boys were many years younger and those who were older had been lost with their fathers in the storm. The winter gloom, the silence of the women and his loneliness drove him to daydreaming, to the creation of a fantasy world. He saw himself, in coming years, stronger and taller than any man, towering over humanity as Cahir Roe towered over the sea, impregnable, aloof. Boats, fields, cattle, houses, everything in the village would belong to him. For as yet the outside world meant nothing to him and women had no power over his dreams. They existed but to serve him.

At first the women paid no more attention to him than they did to the other children. He ate what food was set before him. Some potatoes, a piece of dried salt fish, a bowl of buttermilk. He performed such tasks as were set him, helping with the few cows, carrying the sea-wrack, heeling the turf. Indeed he was despised rather than otherwise, for the girls of his age were more nimble and less absent-minded than he. But slowly, as if in answer to his dreams, his position changed. In every house he entered he was welcomed and given the seat by the fire. He was never allowed to depart without food and drink. The older women baked and cooked for him, kept the best for him, gave him small presents from their hoard: a husband's knife; a son's trousers. They began to compliment him at every turn on his strength and growth. No one asked him to work.

Now he allowed his hair to grow like a man's. The stubby quiff vanished and a crop of thick, fair curls crowned his forehead, giving him the obstinate look of a fierce young ram. He became particular about the cleanliness of his shirt, refused to wear old patched trousers and coats. Gradually he dominated the whole village. Even the dogs owned him sole master, and snarled savagely at one another when he called them to heel. The younger boys were his slaves, to fetch and carry for him. He scarcely noticed the girls of his own age, never called them by name, never spoke directly to them. Unlike them, he had no wish to leave the village.

A day came when Larry Boyle went from house to house and collected the fishing lines, hooks and spinners which had belonged to the drowned men. They were granted him as if by right. He took them to the rock behind the village where formerly the fish had been dried and where the men had then met in the summer evenings to talk, away from their womenfolk. It was a day of shifting sun and shadow and the wind from the west broken by the headland.

He sang as he carefully tested, cut and spliced each line. He rubbed the hooks and spinners clean of rust with wet sand from the stream. He made a long line, tested each length and wound it in a coil between hand and elbow. He fastened the hooks and the lead weight. Then, satisfied, he went down to the shore to dig bait.

He swung his can of bait over his shoulder, picked up his line and made for Cahir Roe. He was going to fish for rockfish.

A deep shelf ran round part of the headland and from this the men had fished in the drowsy heat of summer days when they could spare time from the fields. He clambered along the shelf and stood on the edge. The sea heaved and foamed beneath him. Far out, Tory rose, a castle against the white line of the horizon.

He fixed his bait carefully and placed the loose end of the line beneath his heel. Then, clear of the beetling rock behind, he swung the coil of line above his head and threw it far out. His body, balanced over the edge, seemed to follow it as his eye watched the untwisting of the cord, the drop of the lead towards the sea. He bent down and gathered up the end.

He could feel the movement as the length of line ran through the sea and the weight sank slowly through the heavy water. His hand knew what was happening down there beneath the surface of the water. He felt the lead strike the bottom. His fingers, born to a new delicacy, held the line firmly so that the bait should float free. He could feel the gentle nibbling of the fish at the bait, nibbling cautiously, daintily, as sheep nibble grass. Twice he drew in his line to rebait the hook. Then one struck.

Excited, breathing heavily, his eyes distended, he drew in the line slowly, letting it fall in careful coils at his feet. Then the fish left the water and the full weight hung on the line. It plunged about madly in the air, twisting and flapping. The cord rubbed against the edge of the shelf as it passed from hand to hand, dislodging small stones and dirt from the crumbling surface. He had to lean out to jerk the fish over the edge, at that moment unaware of everything but the twisting, flapping fish. He threw it well behind him so that it could not leap back into the water. It lay there, twisting and turning, its brilliant orange and green colouring coming and going, its belly heaving, its panting gills shining red. Then it lay still and from its open mouth the brick-red blood flowed over the stones. Another leap, another twitch. It was dead.

Larry passed the back of his hand across his forehead to wipe away the sweat. Before he stooped to disengage the hook from the jaws of the fish, he looked around him, at Tory on the far horizon, at the towering cliff above, the heaving sea beneath. For a moment his head reeled as he felt the turning of the world.

The women liked the new schoolmistress. They liked her modesty and reserve. Though young she knew how to keep the children in order, teach them their lessons and their manners. They looked after her with approval when they saw her walk precisely from the school to the cottage where she lived, her hands stiffly by her sides, her eyes lowered. They admired her round, rosy face, her light hair, her neat figure. She appeared so young and lovely to these women whose bodies were lean and tired from hard work and poor food.

She never stopped at the half-door for a chat, nor delayed for a moment to pass the time of day with a neighbour on the road. She never played with the younger children. She walked around encased in herself.

Every Saturday while the road held, she would mount her clean, well-oiled bicycle and cycle to Clonmullen. On the way she did not speak to anyone nor answer a greeting. With gaze fixed on the road before her, she pedalled furiously. In Clonmullen she would make one or two purchases, post her letters and cycle back home. All attempts at conversation were firmly repulsed. She did not even stop to have tea at the hotel.

She lived alone in a small cottage built on the rise of ground just beyond the village. For an hour at a time she would kneel in the shelter of the fuchsia hedge and gaze hungrily at the houses she did not wish to enter, at the women to whom she did not care to speak. She knew all their comings and goings, all the details of their daily life. She watched them at their work, in their conversation. She watched the children at play. She watched Larry Boyle as he wandered along the shore towards Cahir Roe to fish, or passed her cottage on his way to set rabbit snares in the burrows.

The July heat beat down on the earth and the blue-grey sea moved sleepily under a mist. He was returning home when he saw her, standing in the shelter of the bushes that grew over the gateway. She was looking at him with fierce intentness. He stood still and gazed back, his eyes wide and startled. The fear of unknown lands, of uncharted seas took hold of him. His mouth dropped open, his skin twitched. His throat hurt and there was a hammering in his ears like the heavy pounding of the surf on Cahir Roe. He could not move hand nor foot. With a sudden movement her hand darted out and caught his wrist. She drew him towards her, in the shelter of the thick fuchsia hedge. Frightened by her intent stare, her pale face, her quick uneven breathing, when she put out her other hand to fondle him, he pulled away and burst through the bushes. Quietly, with lowered eyes, she listened as his boots clattered over the rocky road. She sighed and turned back into her house.

But he came back. Furtively. He would steal into her kitchen when she was at school and leave some offering: a freshly caught fish, a rabbit, some rock pigeon's eggs. He had so little to give. She did not seem to notice. She did not stop him to thank him when they met. She passed without even a greeting, once again encased in her rigid calm. Then one evening, as darkness fell, he lifted the latch of her door. She was seated on her hearthrug, gazing at the glowing turf fire. He approached in silent desperation and with the same wild desperation she answered.

Such happenings do not long remain hidden in a small world. Without a word spoken, the women came to know. Primitive anger seized hold on them. They said nothing to Larry. Their belief in man's place in life and the fact that they had denied him nothing shut their mouths. All their rage turned against the young teacher whom they had thought so modest and gentle. They became as fierce as hawks at the theft of their darling.

They ceased work. They came together in groups, muttering. They buzzed like angry bees. Their lips spoke words to which their ears were long unaccustomed as they worked themselves into an ancient battle fury. They smoothed their hair back from their foreheads with damp and trembling hands. They drew their small shawls tightly round their shoulders.

From behind the fuchsia hedge the girl saw them coming like a flock of angry crows. Their wide dark skirts, caught by the light summer breeze, bellowed out behind them. Their long, thin arms waved over their heads like sticks in the air. Their voices raised in some primitive battle cry, they surged up the road towards her.

Terrified of this living tidal wave, she rushed out. The uneven road caught her feet. It seemed to her that she made no headway as she ran, that the surging mass of women came ever nearer. Stones rattled at her heels. She ran on in blind panic, unaware of where she was going. Her chest began to ache, her throat to burn. A stone caught her shoulder but she scarcely felt the blow.

Then another hit her on the back and she stumbled. Still she ran on, not daring to look back. A stone struck her head. She reeled and fell. Over the edge of the narrow bog road, down the bank towards the deep watery ditch. Briars caught her clothes. Her hands grasped wildly at the tufts of rough grass. There she lay, half in, half out of the water, too frightened to move or struggle.

When they saw her fall, the women stopped and stood there in the road, muttering. Then they turned back. They burst into her neat little cottage. They threw the furniture about, broke the delft, hurled the pots out of doors, tore the pretty clothes to ribbons. Then they left, still muttering threats, like the sea after storm.

Later, shivering, aching, sick, the girl dragged herself back onto the road. There was no one there now. The flock of crows had gone. She stood alone on the empty road. There was no sound but the lonely call of a moor bird overhead.

The next day Larry, too, left the village.

The war when it came meant little to these women. The explosions of mines on the rocks could not harm them now that there were no men to risk their lives on the water. The aeroplanes which from time to time circled over the coast seemed to them no more than strange birds, at first matter for wonder and then taken for granted. Sometimes the sea washed up an empty ship's boat, some timbers or empty wooden cases. One morning scores of oranges came dancing in on the waves. The children screamed with delight and, not knowing what they were, played ball with them. But since the oranges did not bounce they soon tired of them and left them along the shore to rot. The women only realised that the war could touch them when the supplies of Indian meal ran out.

All that winter storms lashed the coast. Snow whirled around the houses, blotting out the sight of the fierce sea which growled savagely against the headland of Cahir Roe day and night. Not once during the bitter months did the snow melt on the mountains beyond Clonmullen. The wind tore at the ropes which tethered the thatched roofs, rotting and grass-grown from neglect. The north-east wind drove under the doors, roared in the chimneys; it hardened the earth until it was like a stone.

Yet now it seemed that the silence was broken, that terrible silence they had kept in mourning for their dead. Now in the evenings they gathered round one another's firesides. They told stories, old Rabelaisian tales heard when they were children from the old men of the village. Such tales as lie deep in the minds of people and are its true history. Tales of old wars, of great slaughter of men, of the survival of the women and children, of tricks to preserve the race. They told of the Danes and their love of the dark-haired Irishwomen. They laughed quietly and spoke in whispers of the great power of the Norsemen's bodies, of the fertility of their loins.

Over and over again they told the story of the women of Monastir, who, when widowed and alone, lured with false lights a ship to their shore. What matter that their victims were dark-skinned Turks. Their need was great.

The eyes of the women grew large and full of light as they repeated these tales over the dying embers of their fires. A new ferocity appeared in their faces. Their bodies took on a new grace, grew lithe and supple. As the body of the wild goat becomes sleek and lovely in the autumn.

Spring came suddenly. After the weeks of fierce winds and wild seas, followed days of mild breezes and scampering sunshine. The women threw open their doors and stepped out with light hearts. As they cut the sea-wrack for their fields, they called to one another and sang snatches of old songs. Sometimes one or another would stop in her work and look out over the water at the sea-swallows dipping and skimming over the surface of the water, at the black shags as they swam and dived, at old Leatherwing standing in his corner in wait. The older children laughed and shouted as they helped to spread out the wrack on the fields. The younger ones screamed as they ran along the shore and searched under the rocks for crabs. They called and clapped their hands at the sea-pies as they bobbed up and down on the waves.

On and on the children ran, their toes pink in the sea-water. They chattered together like pies over each fresh discovery. They travelled along the shore until they found themselves out on the point of land beside Cahir Roe, facing the open sea. There they stood and looked out to sea from under sheltering hands.

For some minutes they stood and stared. Then in a body they turned and ran towards the women, shouting all together that out there, coming closer every minute, was a strange boat.

The women straightened their backs and listened. Even before they understood what the children were shouting, they let down their petticoats and started for the point. There they stood in a group and stared, amazed that a boat should put in on that inhospitable shore. Close in now, with flapping sail, the boat came.

They could make out only one man and their eyes, used to long searching over water, could see that he was lying across the tiller. Was he alive or dead? Could he not see where he was going? If he did not change his course now he would fetch up on the reef below Cahir Roe. They rushed forward to the water's edge and shouted. The man bent over the tiller did not move. They continued to shout. They waded into the sea until the water surged against their bodies and threatened to overbalance them. Their dark skirts swirled round them in the heavy sea as they shouted and waved their arms.

Then the man at the tiller slowly raised his head. He looked around him, at the sea, at the screaming women, at the great red granite face of Cahir Roe. With great effort he pulled his body upright and swung the tiller over. Then he fell forward again. Even before the keel had grounded on the gravel, the women had seized the boat and dragged it up onto the beach.

Six men lay huddled in the bottom of the boat. Great, strong men, now helpless. The women turned to the helmsman. He looked at them with dull, sunken eyes. He moved. He tried to speak. His grey face was stiff, his lips cracked.

'Scotland?' he asked and his voice was hoarse.

The women shook their heads. Then the man slowly lifted one hand, pointed to the men at his feet and then to himself.

'Danes. Torpedoed. Ten days.'

The women cried aloud as they lifted the heavy bodies of the men. Their voices sang out in wild exultation.

The Danes. The Danes were come again.

Harvesting seaweed, County Clare

Floodtide

MÁIRTÍN Ó CADHAIN 1948

Coming back home to Ireland is the dream of many expatriates, which can become too easily romanticised, as the heroine of this story, a young woman from New York, realises when she returns in the 1940s. Every year the thin soil of the south-western shores needs its carpeting of seaweed without which it lacks the fertility to grow even the most basic of foods. Mairead has to learn anew that the weed must be gathered in obedience to the sea and the demands of those around her.

Mairead shook herself, made a fork of her first and ring-finger to rub the sleepclots from her eyes, felt the early-morning chill on her forearms. Her body took pleasure in her failure to rise. She curled herself back again on the warm side of the bed which Padraig had left a short while ago.

The month since she had come home, together with the three weeks since she had married, had left her out of practice. She thought of those ten years in America when she used to be out on the floor every single morning at the first clockwarning before daybreak for the sake of . . . for the sake of this day – a day when she could either rise or lie abed as she liked.

'Did ye get up yet?' The quavering voice of her mother-in-law, it reached her from the far-room through the door which Padraig had left open behind him.

'We did,' said Mairead, and rubbed some more sleep out of her eyes.

They said, she told herself, that Padraig wouldn't have the tenacity to wait for me until I'd be able to pay their passages over for my three sisters. It was said that since he was 'the only eye in the spud' he would give in to his mother and marry some other woman long ago . . . . It was said that considering how young I was when I went over I'd forget him, marry beyond, and likely . . .

'Get up, Mairead. Lydon will be fit to be tied. The ebb won't wait for anybody . . . .'

She was jerked out of her daydream by the sharpness which she sensed for the first time in the old woman's voice. It proclaimed that the immemorial duel between a man's mother and his wife was about to begin. Having fastened on the bits of clothes that were nearest to her hand in the halfdark she remembered the rumour that was going the rounds, that the old woman was irked by the scant dowry which she had brought into the house. To wait ten years . . . . Put up with a member of the American upper-class and the crumbs that fell from the table . . . . Her shoe-lace broke in half in the second eyelet from the bottom . . . . She felt the first tinge of bitterness.

'It's a long time since anyone got up so early in this house! Spring is at hand, at long last. Now Mairead, a splash of tea would make a gay young man of me.'

Padraig had a fire down, the kettle hissing on the boil, while he brought a handful of oats out to the horse that stood already straddled at the door. With the gaiety in his voice, the love and affection that showed in his face as he named her, Mairead's irritation melted away. For the sake of all this she'd be well able to bear with the old woman's nagging. There'd never be an angry word between herself and Padraig, or if there was she herself would surely be to blame . . . .

It wasn't quite bright as they left home. Down at the Beach Boreen Lydon's two daughters were seated on a pair of upturned basket-creels, while Lydon himself strode up and down at the edge of the shingle gnawing on his pipe.

'Upon my oath,' he said, 'damn the wisp of seaweed I thought'd be cut on the Ridge today! I never yet saw a new-married couple destroyed by a desire to get up.'

The pair of daughters smiled, and Mairead laughed aloud.

'It has ebbed a bit,' said Padraig sheepishly.

'Ebbed a bit! And it almost at low-water! The spring-tide is at the second day of its strength, and unless we seize our chance, today and tomorrow, there'll be no such low-water again this year when it'll be possible to reap the deep seaweed beds of the Ridge.'

'It's a spring-tide,' said Mairead innocently. Having gone to America so early in life she had only a hazy knowledge of some of the home realities whose names were knit into the network of her memory.

'Spring-tide,' said Lydon with the look of a bishop in whose presence an impudent blasphemy has been uttered.

'The Spring-tide of the Feast of St Brigit! You're not acclimatised to the spring-tides yet, girl dear, and they're not exactly what's itching you.'

He winked an eye at her and with a beck of his head drew her attention to

Padraig who was on ahead, going down the shingle slope with Mairead's creel fixed into his own slung from his back.

At this point she didn't feel much like talk, it was enough to have to envisage her share of today's work which lay before her. For a week past the old couple had but the one tune, the Spring-tide. But she hadn't been a bit worried about going to the beach until she found herself now at the edge of the shingle.

She was born and grew up on 'Great Harbour's edge.' She had gathered periwinkles and sandeels, sloke, dulse, carrageen. The spring before she crossed over she had helped her father cut beach-crop. But she had gone before she was fully inured to the hardship of the shore. Soon her hands were wrinkled with washing, scouring, cooking, instead of acquiring the leathery skin of the sea-forager. Those ten years – years in which the sea would have injected its own bitterness into her blood and tempered her bones to its own mettle – she had spent them without setting eyes above ten times on saltwater.

But as they came then to the exposed margin of the ocean the salt wind in from the great waste sharpened her spirit.

'Aren't there many in the neighbourhood,' she said to herself, 'many who spent even twenty years in America and are as used to this hardship today as if they had never left home? What's the hardship of the sea but part of the hardship I'll have to school myself again to? How is it worse than bog-hardship, field-hardship, the hardship of cattle and pigs, the hardship of bearing and rearing if God grants me family . . . .'

At the same time she would have preferred if that section of seaweed on the Ridge wasn't to be gathered in partnership with the Lydons. Would Nora and Caitin Lydon be mocking the ignoramus? Would the tale of her clumsiness come home to her mother-in-law? How well it happened on my first day out that the Ridge had to be harvested in partnership! Pity it's not myself alone and Padraig.

She was determined to do her best for Padraig's sake, but she knew the best he'd allow her would be little enough for fear she'd overstrain herself from lack of practice in the job. If there were only two potatoes in the cow's tub it was 'For God's sake, your back!' from Padraig. Just now Mairead would rather he threw his shyness to the wind and wait to give her a helping hand. She was having great difficulty with the smooth and shifting stones of the shingle which were sliding under her feet and twice as quick to slip the more she tried to tread lightly over them.

'There's a vast difference between this and the streets of New York,' said Lydon as they clattered down to the end of the shingle. 'You should have put on hobnailed boots. You'd do better on the beach barefoot than in those light little toytoys.'

'First thing to my hand this morning,' said Mairead laughing, this time with an effort.

The sand, crisp and firm, on the ebb-strand was such a relief that she made a short dash towards a cluster of whelks and periwinkles which the tide had left stranded overnight. She inserted the toe of her shoe under them and struck Padraig with them on the calf of the leg. But he still didn't wait back for her.

She found it hard going at the place they called 'the footway' between high-water mark and the farthest line of the ebb. Every year, every generation, Lydons and Cades had planned to make a horse-track of this, but it remained 'intention good, performance poor.' She made a good deal of this uncouth passage by taking little leaps clean across the pools. Whenever she was faced with rugged outcrops of rock she slid sideways along them embracing a boulder. Her paps and the rockgrowths both suffered. Once a tentacle of sea-anemone kept her from falling. Once a little kingdom of periwinkles on a rockface went splashing down into the pool. The laughter of the work-party echoed in the clefts and fissures of the shore.

The Ridge was the farthest point out from land: a reef of rock, gapped, polished and bitten into by the ceaseless gnawing of the ocean. The Ridge was never entirely exposed; yet it could be harvested at the ebb of a spring-tide if one took the chance of a wetting. Padraig tucked the ends of his jacket of white homespun into his trouser-band and went to his hips in the narrow channel, but drew back again when he felt himself taken.

'We had better start on this black-weed here,' Lydon said as if venting his ill-humour with the Cades in redirecting it against the slowness of the ebb. 'Isn't that a nuisance now?'

'Not worth our while killing ourselves with a year's growth,' said Padraig, but since everyone else had begun he started himself. It pained Mairead to see the saltwater dripping from his clothes. She glanced towards him again and again so that the look in her eye might let him know how sorry she felt for him, but Padraig never once raised his head. She understood that since the spoils were to be divided equally between the two households, and seeing that there were three Lydons, Padraig was attempting to do two men's work. It didn't take her long to realise he was actually standing in for three: she herself was useless, might as well not be there at all. She was slipping on the slimy rockslabs, while the scabby one-year's growth was so tough that she skinned her knuckles trying to strip it from the rough coating of the stones. No matter how often she sharpened her hack-knife the result was the same. A stalk of seaweed sliced her finger. She stared at the blood dripping on the rock, loath to complain. Until Caitin Lydon noticed it and bound it with a strip of her calico bodice which the saltwater took neatly off again in no time. She felt her fingers numb, dark blue blotches appeared about the joints on the back of her hands. She had to begin rubbing the back of one hand in the crotch of the other. But she wasn't really shamed until she had to go wading.

Padraig glanced at her now and then out of the corner of his eye, vexation in his look, she thought – vexed that on account of the partnership she was obliged to do work which for his part he'd never ask her to do.

'The February bite is in the morning yet,' said Caitin Lydon. 'I suppose you find the beach strange?'

'Ah, not very,' said Mairead.'One has to get used to it, I suppose.'

'It's a sloppy sort of earning,' said Nora Lydon. 'If I was in America, Lord, it's long ere I'd leave it. My passage is coming this summer.'

'You're never without the hard and belittling word for the life at home,' said Caitin to her young sister. 'But perhaps you may sigh for it some day.'

Caitin spoke in the adult tone of a housewife, heir to the Lydon house, land and strand. But it seemed to Mairead that somewhat more than the mere defence of the homelife caused the sting in her voice. It was on the tip of Mairead's tongue to tell her about the shopkeeper in Brooklyn who had been pressing her to marry him until the day she left America; however, she refrained. It would be a matter for mockery in all the visiting-houses of the village that night. Did ever a slut or a slattern come back from America who hadn't some millionaire or other asking to marry her beyond?

By now the men had succeeded in getting out on the Ridge by going waist-deep in the water but the women stayed where they were until it had ebbed more in the channel.

Lydon, out on the Ridge, kept up a constant stream of orders back to his own daughters – strip the stones down to the skin – they wouldn't be reaped again for a couple of years. But Mairead was well aware he was aiming at her, though his eye never once lit on her. Soon the women moved out across the

channel towards a red sand newly exposed near the last of the ebb. Mairead
stood watching a crab that flopped about in a pool till he went in under a
slanting stone. It gave her her best to dislodge the stone, but what came out of
it but a tiny speckled fish that escaped her grasp and went into a cleft between
two thighs of rock. Her heart jerked. She thought of the lusty appetite for
crabs and rockfish she had when a girl. Her father had never come home from
a seaweed-strand without bringing back some beach-gatherings. If Padraig
wasn't so busy she'd ask him to collect her a hank of crabs and rockfish. The
slab beside her was architected all over with limpets. She had a keen thought
of the rare occasions she had served limpets and cockles as a tasty titbit in
America, but she wouldn't give tuppence for that manner of serving
compared with a batch of shellfish roasted on the embers. She began to long
for the limpets. Maybe, too, they might sweeten the humour of the old
woman at home. She thrust her blade in under the edge of a limpet that was
slightly detached from the stone. She was reluctant at first to interfere
between it and the rock. In spite of herself she was thinking of her
mother-in-law going between herself and Padraig. But the limpet came away
so readily with her that she had no further scruple. Pity I haven't a little can or
a bucket, she thought. Then she remembered the apron she had on over her
American dress, if she gathered it up and tied it behind it would hold a fine lot.
She could put them in the creel when work on the beach was over. Bit by bit,
she told herself, I am getting the knack of the shore.

'It's not worth bothering yourself with those limpets, Mairead,' said
Lydon. 'There's twice the sustenance in the top-shore limpet than in the
low-water one, and anyhow the limpet is never at his prime till he has taken
three drinks of April water.'

Though what he said was true, she took the hint that it wasn't to pick
limpets she came but to cut seaweed.

She made her way out farther along with the two women. She was attracted
by the little sand-pools left by the last of the ebb. Her thoughts were seduced
by the faint thrum of the wave in the channel-mouth and the ripples of brine
breaking in white flakes on the miniature strand made her happy in herself
so that she lay into the work. Nor did she find it so piercingly difficult.
Though the commonest weed here was the sawtooth wrack there was a lush
growth of black-weed here and there on the backs of the jagged scarps, with
patches of top-shore seaweed in among it and luxurious bunches of
yellow-weed that were like golden tresses of hair in the rays of the morning

sun. She was keener to go at them than she had been with the limpets a short while ago.

Now Lydon's tone began to grow sharp:

'Of course, ladies, ye don't imagine that old coarse-crop field of mine back up there is able to digest sawtooth wrack! Every single stalk of it will be still in the earth in its own shape next autumn. It isn't as if I'd ask you your business if it was sowing the loam at the bottom of the village I was. The tidewater is shallow enough now for you to come out here.'

Caitin Lydon went out barefoot as far as a boulder under the Ridge. Nora took her boots off and got out on to another slab. Mairead did likewise with her own shoes. About to hoist up her skirt she hesitated once or twice and glanced shamefaced towards Lydon and Padraig. All she had under it was a transparent American petticoat. It surprised her at first how unconcerned the other pair were about hoisting a skirt, until she remembered they had never left home. Her feet shrank from the cold water, she went as gingerly as a cat crossing a patch of wet.

Suddenly she was afraid, the turbulent sea breaking in white spume over the lip of rock in the channel might sweep her legs from under her. The soles of her feet tingled on the gravelly bottom. She tensed her lips, it seemed to her the Lydons were grinning. She looked longingly out towards Padraig, he had his back to her, shearing as furiously as chance offered in the maw of the wave. He never as much as lifted his head . . . .

She was out now on the exposed Ridge in face of the beds of strapwrack. The rank fronds of it excited her greed. She felt a lust to plunder. A desire to strip the rockfaces clean as a plate. She took pleasure in the squeak of the long ribbons of it letting go their hold and the hiss of the sheaves falling in the rock hollows. In spite of the chill and drench of the saltwater she felt a prick in her pulse, a prick ten years absent . . . . She came to a gentle nook sheltered in under the backbone of the Ridge, where there was a feathery growth of carrageen on the cheek of the stone. How often the tuft of carrageen which Nora Sheain Liam brought to America had sent her thoughts bounding to 'Great Harbour's edge', to the dear beach where lay her heart's desire . . . . Again remembering her mother-in-law, she turned aside to pick the carrageen.

'Ladies,' said Lydon, and now the ocean's urgency was in his voice, 'you are proving yourselves none too good. This reef isn't half-reaped yet. How shy you are of wetting yourselves! Saltwater never did harm to anybody.'

Mairead gave up the carrageen, though the voice of Lydon caused her no irritation now. Now she felt sure she was fit to do her share, sure that the ocean's temper was getting under her own skin and through her veins the harsh reality was pulsing.

Again came the warning voice of Lydon:

'It's on the turn! Look, Carrigavackin almost submerged. Hadn't the ladies better begin drawing? They're more suited to that just now.'

For the first time today Padraig raised his head and looked Mairead in the eye. He was on the verge of saying something, but shut his lips up tight again without speaking. Mairead understood, clearly he would forbid her that labour if he could. The strong bond of the partnership had inhibited the affection showing in his eye that moment. He needn't worry. She intended to show that though she might appear to be soft-spun there was a tough weft in her too. Since he was so good to her she was going to put herself to the limit for his sake.

They began filling from the part farthest out. They'd still be able to collect the nearer part until the tide had come well in.

For hands that had been ten years in the sweltering heat of a narrow kitchen it was pure refreshment to feel the stiff slime of the seaweed sticking to them as she stuffed the creel full to the brim. She had no great difficulty with the first creel in spite of the ruggedness of the passage while the brine streamed from the seaweed down along her back.

She put as much top-load on the second creel as did either of the Lydons. Very likely she wouldn't have slipped only that a sheaf of the top-load which overhung the edge of the creel slid off as she cleared the end of the Ridge. But though she slipped she wasn't injured. She grasped a rock which was right at her back and kept such a grip on the creel that only a few sheaves fell off the top. She would have preferred if the two Lydons had gone on instead of leaving their creels on the stones and coming back to help her gather the fallen sheaves. After the third creel it seemed to her that the Lydons were dawdling to allow her to keep up. The spreading-bank was nine or ten yards above high-water mark; the plod up there from the low-water edge seemed to grow longer with every creel. Like trying to teem out a fulltide, she thought.

She was sweating all over, felt the warm trickles of sweat tempering the chill of the saltwater. The strap began to raise blisters on her palms, the brine was biting into the crease of her fingers. Her back was bent stiff, and as for her legs, well, better forget them. They seemed to belong to someone else, not the legs of the one who had come down the boreen so quick and lithe that morning. Afraid every minute she'd turn an ankle. The soles had lifted clean from her light shoes. Every time she trod on a sharp pebble she clenched her foot, arching the instep against the shoe-laces. She was like a horse with a nail in the quick, lifting her foot from a pointed periwinkle or a limpet shell. She was also ravenously hungry. She hadn't eaten much that morning. For ten years she had been in the habit of a cup of tea in the hand at 11 o'clock every day. But fasting was child's play in comparison with this excruciating work. In America there was a break or a change of occupation after every stint. But the selfsame journey, from low-water to the top of the beach, again and again . . . .

Lydon's temper was shortening step by step with the rising tide.

'You are slow, ladies! It seems we'll have to leave this reef uncut and go drawing ourselves. If we're depending on you the floodtide will take a share of what we've already cut.'

Once the men began drawing, the pace grew fiercer. The rugged beach didn't cost them a thought, no more than it did Caitín Lydon who was able to keep up with them barefoot step for step. More often than not Padraig was emptying his creel on the spread-bank by the time the others had reached the tidemark, with Mairéad still not beyond the edge of the sand.

There was no feeling left in her feet. Sometimes when she came to the upper edge of the sand she shut her eyes awhile so as not to be pierced by the prospect of the final stretch. She was dead to all sense of pain by now. She plodded along as if there was someone inside her goading her on. If her body was numb her mind was more so. Nothing occurred to her except disconnected scraps of thought . . . the partnership . . . if the seaweed was left to Padraig and myself . . . a body must become inured to the hardship . . . the floodtide . . . .

She slackened now on the slope of the shingle without strength or will to open her eyes properly. First thing she knew she was into the tidemark, the heap of shells and periwinkles, oozy tangles of oarweed root, bits of board encrusted with barnacles, ringlets of wrack and trash-heaps of red seaweed which had come up with the full of the spring-tide from where it had been rotting during the neap. It was on a slimy strand of redweed she slipped. Quite aware of the feet sliding from under her, she let them go. A relief to let the strap of the creel slip from her grasp . . . . Padraig refilled the creel, took it to the finish.

The eyes of the Lydon girls seemed to her to smile, in spite of what they had to say of . . . treacherous stones . . . too long a distance . . . .

To think she had left the comfort of America for the sake of this. Yet Padraig wasn't to blame for it.

'No need for you to go down any more, Mairead,' said Lydon. 'The three of us will gather what's left out there at a single go, and it'll be no trouble to your boss-man to gather a little creel of the floating weed down at the channel. Padraig lad, hurry, the flood won't have a clump left.'

But now Mairead was determined to go back down. How well they wouldn't ask Nora or Caitin Lydon to stay up here? She'd go down if only to spite them. If that floating weed contained only a single clump she'd make two halves of that clump! She had made her bed and she'd lie on it . . . .

In spite of his striding haste she kept up with Padraig on the way down and when they reached low-tide mark she was no more out of breath than he was. It was some satisfaction that she had Padraig to herself for the fist time since they had come to the beach. She gave up the idea of gathering her share of the floating weed into her own creel; there wasn't the full of a creel in it all told.

Floodtide was now so fiercely breaking in that it seemed to regret having been caught out that morning and intended to take full revenge for having bared at all. It pushed into the channel nuzzling the little piles of stones with its cold snout, sniffing into fissures with its nostrils hissing, feeling its way far up along the ebbway of red sand with its long greedy tentacles, making ravenous attacks on the cut swathes of weed not yet collected. It had already taken a few substantial heaps and Padraig was put to his knees trying to save a clump of strapweed from its gullet.

The rage and rapacity of the sea was in tune with Mairead's turbulent mood. The rush of the surf was an ease to her agonised spirit as it tousled the sawtooth wrack on the stones and broke them despondently, not having yet displaced the little pad of sand the ebb had left. But hardly had the little scattered rills of the first wave been absorbed by the sand when the thrust of the next wave was come to dislodge the wee strip once and for all. Mairead stood in a cold pool on bare-strand edge till the reflux of the wave which had taken the sand-pad drenched her up to the knees. A swimming-crab came out of a crevice and went foraging down the sloping shoulders of the wave. A periwinkle went from the rock as if in a game of tip-and-come with the upsurge of seawater which made a rush for the last gatherings of weed. Out went Mairead into the mouth of the surf to retrieve a clump – a glistening clump of yellow-weed.

'Out of my way!' said Padraig and went to his thighs to snatch the last of the plunder from the devouring tide. Mairead straightened, her mind flared up at that voice. A harsh alien voice. A voice from a law of life other than the life of his complaining letters, other than the life of beguiling and sweethearting, alien to the life of the pillow. With the stab she got the little bladder of seaweed burst between her fingers and squirted a dull slime up in her cheek.

The dark shade she saw on Padraig's features at that moment was as strange and forbidding as the black streaks which the freshening wind was making in the bristling mane of the floodtide . . . .

In Belfast, 1910

The Passing of Billy Condit

SAM McAUGHTRY 1970

Protestant and Catholic have been separate political and religious groupings in Ireland for centuries; they were certainly so long before the island was divided into the Irish Free State and Ulster in 1922. In this story, set in 1885, these same divisions occur in a poor area of the city of Belfast. The major industries, linen and shipbuilding, were controlled by the ruling Protestant group who would employ no Catholics, except in menial jobs. A worker showed loyalty by respect to the British monarch and by marching in the processions organised by the Orangemen – so called after William of Orange, whose victory over Irish Catholics in 1690 has been celebrated on 12 July ever since. Marriages between Catholics and Protestants were very unusual and were frowned on by the leaders of both communities. But there have always been people like Mary Condit who have struggled to maintain their independence.

Like the city, the street was young, in 1885. It was steep and narrow, running down to the very perimeter of the harbour estate. It overlooked the cranes and gantries, the spars of coastal sailing vessels, and the upperworks of steamers, moored by newly-built wharves.

In mid-morning there were no men to be seen, only the occasional shawled woman walking, head down. The children in the school at the top of the street chanted multiplication tables. The heavy stamp of a draught horse, and the crash of iron-rimmed wheels on cobblestones carried through the kitchen door, to where Mary Condit was on her knees.

Her long black hair was caught and tied at the back of her neck. When a strand fell out of place she would throw her head back and push the hair away from her eyes with a hand that was guttered from the floor's dirt.

Lizzie was at work in the mill on York Street, and Hugh was at school. The boy would come round the corner in an hour, for his lunch. Through the kitchen window the finished washing could be seen on the line in the yard. Her husband's rough flannel working shirts were pegged alongside long, grey drawers, pummelled and knuckled on the washboard an hour earlier. The tuppenny bone for the supper broth, the vegetables and peeled potatoes, were ready in their pots on the hob.

Rim-high in the bowls, the broth would be served when Billy Condit sat down, shining pink clean, after his wash at the scullery sink. Mary scrubbed the kitchen floor contentedly. The day was going with no fuss. At seven in the evening it would reach its high point when the family, the four of them, sat down to supper.

When Mary was growing up in this street her mother, with eight people packing the tiny kitchen, had eaten on the move, spooning food from a saucer as she stirred and ladled and handed out helpings. But at seven o'clock Mary would sit opposite Billy, with Hugh and Lizzie in between. There would be time for talk. She would see her man's face, newly-shaved, and on the bare chest the breast-curls, and the silken line that ran from broad to narrow: from chest to navel. And when he caught her looking he would wink . . . .

Beside Mary on the floor was a large paint tin. It was half filled with black, soft soap. She scooped some of this on to the tip of the scrubbing brush and scoured the red, rough tiles. The fumes from the soap could bring tears to the eyes. She scrubbed in loops and whirls, rinsed and dried, then stood, wiping her hands on the sacking apron that she wore. Carrying the bucket, she stepped out into the yard.

Opposite the scullery pipe outlet, Mary bent and lifted the hem of her heavy skirt. Pulling her knickers down below the knees, she crouched. Her water ran down the slope of the yard and gurgled into the grating, carrying with it part of the brown-yellow beard of tea leaves that rimmed the gulley's edge. The woman idly watched the course of the water. Her eyes lifted, and, suddenly, with a half scream, she stood, clutching at her clothing, turning away from the face that watched, just visible over the edge of the wall. Knees together, tucking vest under knickers, she hurtled to the kitchen door, away from the wide, watching eyes.

The face wore a grey moustache that hung wetly down the sides of the mouth: 'Ya dirty oul blirt ye, Johnny Millar,' Mary yelled, hopping from foot to foot, straightening her clothes. The long thin face slid down out of sight. A voice that was high and nasal was heard: 'I was only looking for my canary that got out.'

'I'll canary ye, ya oul get ye. If ya want to look at a woman why the hell don't ya get married.' Restored to decency, Mary came back out into the yard, ducking under the clothes line: 'By God but when my man comes home the night I'll not be long in telling him about you, ya bloody oul whoremaster.'

From the other side of the wall the thin voice was heard: 'Dick? Come here, Dick. Where are ye, son?'

Back inside, Mary scrubbed her hands in the scullery. The annoyance gradually died from her face, to be replaced by the twitch of a smile. There was no sense in telling Billy. All the other times, he'd only smiled: 'I only wish I was as easily pleased,' he'd said, 'it's a hell of a cheap way to get your satisfaction, you have to admit it. My appetite costs me my week's wages.'

She was drying her arms when there came a sudden knock at the front door. She went into the hall. On the step was a man, a tall stranger. In his fifties, sour-featured, he wore a navy blue, shiny suit, and a black, hard hat. His high, starched collar bit into the undersides of his jowls:

'Are you Missus . . .?' He paused, peering at a scrap of paper in his hand: '. . . Condit?' Mary nodded, bowing her head respectfully, for his tone was one of authority.

'Well?' Impatiently, 'Can I come in, then?'

Pulling the sleeves of her cardigan down over her bare arms, Mary pushed back against the kitchen door, as the man went into the house ahead of her. 'I'm just after washing the floor,' she said, shyly. Frowning, the visitor's gaze followed hers. Seeing the paint tin, he stooped and lifted it. Dipping a finger into it, he held it close to his nose and sniffed: 'Was that soap lifted out of the yard?'

His dentures fitted badly, puffing his upper lip out. His eyes, watching her, were narrowed. Flustered, the woman's face flamed: 'No, mister.'

It had, in fact, come from the shipyard. Every time a ship was launched the slipways were covered in a mixture of crude soap and engine oil, and after the launch the workmen scooped it into tins and carried it home, with the knowledge of the foremen. The soap was so strong that it stung the hands. It was fit only for scrubbing floors.

Mary's face paled. She looked from the soap to the man, afraid to meet his gaze, rubbing her hands on the sacking tied round her waist.

'You can get yourself into serious trouble, taking shipyard property,' the stranger said, sternly. His voice had the Scots harshness of North Antrim. It was a familiar sound to Mary. Belfast, doubling and redoubling in size, growing in prosperity, was sucking in the coastal people in tens of thousands. Mary herself belonged to a Carrickfergus, Co. Antrim family, only one generation in the city.

The man made to point his finger at Mary, and suddenly noticed the paper in his hand. He cleared his throat: 'Is William Condit, hand riveter in the Queen's Island, your man?'

'He's my man, mister, but he never took the soap. My wee girl got it from a woman in the mill.'

'For dear sake, missus, I'm not talking about the soap.' The man's expression was almost contemptuous: 'I'm here to tell you what happened at the White Star boat this morning.' He looked again at the paper: 'Your man fell off the staging. He fell forty feet.'

Mary was still. Her hands fell to her sides.

'He broke his neck.' The stranger's eyes were fixed on the wall behind and above Mary's head: 'He's dead. He's in the City Morgue.'

Her first feeling was one of relief. The man wasn't talking any more about the soap. Then, for the first time since he had come into her house, she looked him full in the face, questioning, searching.

He stood watching her. He kept sucking his teeth, pushing at the dentures with the inside of his lip. Suddenly he turned to the door. Mary followed, her head shaking slightly. At the step he adjusted his hard hat: 'You have a boy, they say?' She nodded.

'Usually, when this happens, the first son gets preference. But there's a question here about religion. I can't promise anything.' He glanced past Mary through the open door, and saw the tin of soap on the floor. Shaking his head irritably, he walked quickly down the street, buttoning his jacket, not looking back.

Watching him, Mary's hand sought support from the doorpost.

The street was still and quiet, except for the tiny slap of the red, white and blue bunting that hung in rows all the way down to the docks. Immediately outside the Condit's house hung a huge portrait of Queen Victoria. Under it were the words: 'God Save Our Queen. No Home Rule.'

It was the central feature of the street's Twelfth of July decorations. Ever since Mary and Billy had come to live there, in 1870, fifteen years earlier, they'd hung the Queen's portrait outside their house.

As a reminder.

She had the place to herself. She dug the nose of the scrubbing brush viciously into the pitted scullery tiles, and twisted the cloth so fiercely that it reared in her hands like a snake, until the last drop of water was wrung from it. The scullery didn't need washing. It had been done over half a dozen times since Billy had been taken, in his coffin, to the new cemetery near Glengormley, under the shadow of Ben Madigan. That was a week ago but still the sweet flower scent clung. The whole house was full of the smell of carbolic soap, but still it wasn't enough to drown the camphor from the priest's vestments, the new-varnished pine smell.

Mary stood, rubbing her bare knees to ease the smarting. She opened the yard door and emptied the bucket into the grating. Back in the kitchen she sighed. There was still the fire to be laid.

On the first morning of their married life Billy had laid the fire, and for every day of his life after, he'd made it up for her, leaving the hearth clean and shining for Mary to come down to. She'd never quite grown used to the luxury of it. She was standing, looking at the untidy grate, when there was a light tap on the kitchen door, and Kathleen Johnstone came in.

'You haven't got a wee taste of physic, have you, love?' Kathleen took her usual seat on the sofa, opposite the yard window: 'It's wee Tommy,' she said, 'he's not at himself, and his tongue's all white, like.' Her gaze shifted from the window to the dresser by the door, back to the window. She looked down at the ragged, canvas slippers on her feet.

Mary was at the cupboard beside the mantelpiece: 'I've some seeney pods left.' She handed the other woman a thin, paper bag. As she did so, she glanced shrewdly at her: 'What was it you did want, Katie?'

They'd been friends since childhood, working at adjoining looms in the York Street factory. And one lunch-time the two girls had been part of the crowd cheering the Inniskillin Fusiliers, in their brass and regimentals, newly returned from India, marching behind their pipes to Victoria Barracks when, behind them, Billy Condit and Alex Johnstone, on their meal hour from the shipyard, had begun to tease the pair of them.

That had been fifteen years earlier. Now Kathleen, with six children, was Mary's neighbour. Small and stout, with sleeves rolled up and hair in a bun, she could have passed for Mary's sister. In the first years of their married lives the two had many times agreed that they'd been lucky that day on York Street, meeting men who'd brought their pay home, and caused no worry.

Kathleen sighed: 'There's more trouble, love.'

'What way, trouble?'

The kitchen door from the street opened and Hugh came in. Small, finely built, he had the black hair and brown eyes of his parents. His jersey and knee-length trousers sat neatly on him. The boy sat down beside Kathleen, who gave his ear an affectionate tweak: 'There's a wee boy's in for a piece and jam, and then he's wanting straight out again, isn't that right, Hugh?'

Hugh looked from one to the other: 'So that's the way of it?' His voice was clear and carrying, like his father's. 'That's the way of it,' he said, 'I've to let yez get on with your talking, have I?'

Kathleen gave the boy a quick hug. 'You've a quare wise head on them shoulders,' she said.

Mary had cut a thick slice of home-baked bread and was covering it with salted, country butter, bought from farm carts in the street. Hugh came and stood beside her as she spread jam on it, and handed it to him. The boy's eyes sought hers, but she was staring at Kathleen Johnstone, a frown on her face. He ran out into the street again.

'It's about Hugh,' Kathleen said. 'Him going to the Star of the Sea school with the other sort.' She was looking down at her hands. 'The way you're rearing him, you know?' She stood up and walked to the door. 'Alex was told in the shipyard. There's some big man from the Orange coming to see you. I think Alex was told on purpose, with him being a friend of your Billy's. So that it would get to you.' She looked down at the senna pods in her hand. 'I'll have to be getting back, so I will.'

When Hugh came back Mary was still looking at the open door: 'Have you finished all your secret talking?' He winked his father's wink. Mary gave a sudden smile and pulled him down on to the sofa. 'Are the wee boys in the street leaving you alone?' she asked, tossing his hair, then straightening it.

'Aw they don't bother me,' he said, 'anyway, they're not annoying me since my daddy died.' He squirmed away from her, knelt at the fire. 'Do you want me to fix the fire for you?'

He rolled up his sleeves, as tears filled Mary's eyes.

'Excuse me for asking,' Mary said, 'but how well did you know my man?'

The Orangeman crossed and uncrossed his legs. One leg of his long, white drawers showed, tucked into the top of a thick woollen stocking. He studied his brown boots. 'Well,' uncomfortably, 'I didn't actually know him. Not as a friend, like.'

'Do you work in the shipyard, then?'

'No, I'm at the docks, myself. Cross Channel.'

He was a well-paid craneman. The Protestants worked the cross-Channel boats, the Catholics did heavier, poorly-paid work at the deep-sea sheds.

'I see. You don't – didn't – know Billy. You didn't work with him, but you're sorry for my trouble. Well, it's very good of you, Mister. Do you live round here?'

'Well, I live down the Shore Road.'

'It's very good of you.' Mary moved to the door, opened it.

The Orangeman stood. He was angry with himself for feeling awkward, but this woman had taken him by surprise, standing there, quiet and calm. Dignified, even.

She must have been bloody good-looking as a girl. It must have been one powerful shock to her people, when she came home and said she was for marrying one of the left-footers. He twisted his cap into a crescent, turned it over in his hands: 'What I called about was the wee fellow.'

This call had been his own idea. To impress the retired colonel who had taken the chair at the District Lodge meeting.

From the Grand Lodge, the colonel was. He'd explained about Gladstone getting in, but needing the 86 Irish Nationalists. So the Government was talking about a Home Rule Bill: 'That's if we're stupid enough to let them,' the colonel had said. Then he'd explained that it took time for a Bill to become an Act: 'It's time we must use,' he said.

Later in the meeting the talk had come round to the death of the Catholic hand riveter. Behind hands, it was described as the first Home Rule protest. So, since he'd not known enough to join in the debate about Home Rule, the District Secretary had said that there was a Protestant mother and a Catholic son, and that he'd call and put the mother right on some things. 'Sounds like a jolly good idea,' the colonel had said.

'Do you not think you should rear the wee fella in your own church?' the Orangeman asked. He was, somehow, standing on the pavement. 'I believe your wee girl's Church of Ireland, like yourself. Why not the wee fella, now that . . . ?'

'You mean, now that they've killed his father?'

He unrolled his cap, put it on his head. He was low-set and stocky. His shirt front sat out from his high-buttoned jacket, as though there was an extra garment underneath. 'You can't say you weren't warned,' he said, and turned to go.

Mary's voice stopped him. 'You hadn't the bloody neck to come and say that when my man was alive.' Her voice was low, and steady. 'You chicken-chested wee blirt ye, he'd have put ye on yer bloody back.

'Go you back and tell the Orange that the whole lot of them put together wouldn't make shitehouse paper for my Billy's arse. Now take yourself off.'

Across the street Beeny Mills stood, arms folded high over breasts pushed up by her stays. Beeny's man had been lost when a locally owned ship, half sail, half steam, had foundered with all hands in the North Atlantic two years earlier. Middle-aged, she was childless. After her day in the mill she practically lived at her front door. As the Orangeman walked down the street, mouthing bitter words, Beeny smiled over at Mary. 'I don't know what you were saying there, love, but you look as if it was doing you good.'

'It was, Beeny, it was,' Mary waved as she closed the kitchen door. Once inside, she took the sofa cushions on which the Orangeman had sat, walked with them to the yard, and flung them on the roof of the shed to air.

Lizzie and Hugh were in the house with Mary when the priest called. It was early evening. Mary had been cutting vegetables for the next day's supper when the knock came. Lizzie, in the long, grey frock run up from cotton remnants that she wore to work, took the scullery duties over from her mother. Hugh was sitting on the sofa, idly drawing on his school slate. He jumped to fetch a chair for the priest, who came straight to the point.

'I was talking to the children in the Star of the Sea today about these Twelfth of July decorations, and pictures of the Queen.'

He had the hard, flat vowels of South Armagh. His thighs were thick on the chair. His red neck contrasted with the white of his Roman collar. Dandruff sat on his oily hair, and lay scattered on his shoulders. He glanced to where Mary sat, in a good black dress, by the table. 'I see they've honoured you, as usual, with the setpiece of the display.' She gave only a dry smile in reply.

'Queen Victoria is described on coins, and on Orange pictures, as the Defender of the Faith. But, as I told the children today – didn't I, Hugh? – the Queen doesn't defend the Catholic faith. We must do that for ourselves. That's the reason for my visit, Missus Condit. That's why I'm here. To defend the faith.'

There was only the scratching of Hugh's chalk on the slate. In the scullery Lizzie listened, stirring bone and vegetables on the hissing, new-fangled gas stove.

The priest moved irritably. She hadn't even offered a cup of tea. He glanced around the neat room. There wasn't one holy picture, hadn't been, even when Condit had been here. He'd been the independent sort, held his own views on politics, was neither Nationalist nor Loyalist. Went to the Protestant church and took part in the confirmation service for his daughter, knowing that it was against Catholic teaching. There were others like him in Belfast, too. Funny, how the mixing of the two faiths caused this independence of thought in both parties. Odd. It couldn't please the Protestant church, either.

'I've called to make sure that you intend to keep the promise to the Church,' the priest said.

'What promise to what church?'

He sighed: 'Your late husband, God be with him, undertook to rear the boy as a Catholic. I'm here to remind you, in these sad circumstances, of his promise, and your duty.' His lips tightened. 'Do you follow me?'

'Oh Christ aye, I can follow you all right.' Mary slapped the top of the mantelpiece in emphasis. 'Mind you, before Billy died, I wouldn't have been much good at talking up to men come to see me. But I've had a couple of right specimens in here in the last lot of days, I'm telling you. And you're number three. And between you you've helped me one hell of a lot to follow things.'

The priest shot a glance at Hugh, scribbling industriously, and Lizzie, whose head only could be seen, bent over the saucepans.

'I would think you'll likely be the the last of the men. There couldn't be any more left in the world like yez. Before the first one called the only man that I could tackle was oul Johnny Millar next door, but he was aisy. All he wanted was to watch me going to the yard. But now? Now, there's no man can frighten me. None.'

Mary turned her head towards the scullery: 'Lizzie?'

The girl came into the kitchen. She was flushed from the heat of the stove. The black ringlets at her forehead were moist. She was an inch taller than her mother, with the full figure of a grown woman, and the candid eyes of early youth. 'Yes, mammy?'

'Tell us again what they did on ye in the mill the day.'

The girl gave a resigned smile: 'They made me stand in front of the Queen's picture and sing God Save our Noble Queen.'

'Did they ill-treat you, girl?' The priest's voice was sharp. Lizzie had come close to Mary. Her mother put an arm around her. 'You let me worry about that,' she said.

'It's the times we're living in, Missus Condit.'

'And just who do you think makes the times, then?'

'I'm not sure I know what you mean.'

'Four days ago I had an Orangeman in here telling me it was my duty to rear Hugh as a Protestant. It seems to me that, as far as my family's concerned, it's you and that Orangeman's making the times we're living in.'

The priest stood up and walked to the dresser by the door. He felt better on his feet. He stared levelly down at the woman. 'My duty is clear. I am here to see that your husband's promise to the Church is kept. It's as straightforward as that. Indeed, I'm surprised that I should have to repeat it, considering the circumstances of Mister Condit's passing.'

Mary motioned the priest to the front step. Closing the kitchen door behind her, she jabbed a finger in his chest. His eyes narrowed angrily. 'Look you, priest,' Mary said, 'my man made no promises to any church. The promise was between him and me. We said that we'd keep our own churches, and that our childer would share in that. You've nothing to do with it.'

'Does Hugh stay in the church?'

The priest's eyes were almost closed. 'He does, but only because my man wanted it. And I'll tell you something else we promised. They can either stay in their churches or change churches or give up their churches altogether, now that they're both over twelve it's up to them. It's not up to you or any bloody Orangeman.'

The priest nodded. 'It's an odd way to bring up children, but my work's done for the present. Good day to you. God be good in your trouble.' He walked up the street, tucking the long strands of his hair under the brim of his little, flat priest's hat.

Over at her door, Beeny Mills chuckled, and hitched at her bosom. 'One way and the other, you're having the time of it. I seen the time you couldn't have found a word for them big men.'

'As you said the other day, it's doing me good,' Mary said, closing the kitchen door.

The family sat around the table. The broth things had been pushed to the one side. Hugh sat where his father had sat.

'Well, wee uns, we'll have to go and live with the Catholics.' Mary sipped tea from a thick mug. She looked relaxed. She smiled at the two young ones.

'It'll be a relief going to some other school,' Hugh said. 'I'm fed up the way everybody looks at me.'

'You tell me who's annoying you,' Lizzie said, making a fist. 'I'll hit them a dig on the gub, so I will.'

'What about you and the mill?' Mary said.

'Well, I don't mind singing God Save the Queen,' Lizzie said.

'Unless the mill has changed its way of going,' Mary said, drily, 'you'll be getting the sack if you're up before the Queen's picture any more.'

Hugh was trying to keep a straight face: 'Do you know what we call the priest in school?'

'No, what?' The two women had drawn together.

'Sure you won't hit me?'

'No, go on.'

'Well, we call him oul empty trousers.' Hugh's laughter burst out of him, the women squealed their appreciation, and rude, hearty laughter was heard in the house for the first time since the passing of Billy Condit.

'Hugh here'll have to look after us, when we go to live there,' Lizzie added, giggling.

Hugh held a fist up: 'You tell me who's annoying you and I'll hit them a dig on the gub,' he said.

And outside the bolted door, all up and down the street, the red, white and blue bunting, caught in a sudden breeze, danced and chattered and whispered spitefully, as the young, strong city made ready for religious riot and commotion.

Men of the South by Sean Keating

The Talker

SEÁN LUCY 1972

Over the centuries many idealists struggled for the creation of an independent Irish state. Their dream was partially realised in 1922, after the War of Independence, with the creation of the Irish Free State. The war was fought in all parts of Ireland. This story is set in Cork where the idealistic Con is easily drawn into the fight. But then he discovers the price he has to pay, in his love for Stephanie and his service to his country.

Con Brady was known by the other men in his company as 'the Talker', but the name was a compliment rather than a sneer, because talking was his job.

There would be a meeting in the dark kitchen of a mountainy farm and the plans for the next raid or ambush would be discussed. William Burke, the Commandant, thick-set and dark, would listen to the swift speech of the younger men and then, slowly and with certainty, he would shape a complete, trustworthy plan in the active minds of the others. Afterwards he would turn to Con.

'Con, boy, we don't know what that platoon of the Essex is doin' in Ballingeary. They may be wise to us. Will you try an' find out, lad?'

Con had this job because of his college education: his ability to appear the semi-anglicised West Briton. Also, he looked anything but a rebel – a gangling youth with fair hair and a way of looking you straight in the face while he told the most atrocious lies. He would turn up at the danger spot riding a bicycle and wearing a bowler and gloves: the young Cork city clerk out for the day. He also carried an umbrella strapped to his cross-bar. No Englishman will suspect disloyalty in the possessor of gloves and an umbrella.

He would dismount in the village street and walk up to the officer standing uneasily near his men – men who formed little suspicious groups in the silent roadway.

'Nice day, Captain. Your men look a smart lot. Hope this doesn't mean any damned rebels in the area?'

'No, just routine. I don't expect trouble. Still you never know with those bastards. Got to be bloody careful.'

'Well, you men are doing a fine job. It's nice to see you keeping an eye on things. Cigarette? We'll soon have these rebels put down with your help. Only a bunch of hooligans against you. The Irish people disown them really, you know.'

'Still, they get a lot of passive help round the country. It would be easier for us if there weren't so much sympathy.'

'Well, let's hope it will soon be over. I must be off. Got to be in Cork before curfew, you know. I suppose you'll be going to Macroom for the night?'

'Yes, we move in half an hour. Nice to meet someone friendly. Good luck.'

'Good luck.'

In summer the mountains, tall around the road, shook in the heat as the straggling villages dropped behind. Dust and warm smells of gorse and heather. In the winter, mud, mist and thin rain. But always the farm again and Burke's curt: 'Well?'

'Two platoons under a captain, sir. Two lorries. Returning to Macroom. That should make our way to Skibb clear.'

'Fine. We'll go tonight. But I've another job for you, Con, boy. Go up to the City tomorrow. There's a rumour that new troops are arriving, and I don't trust Hegarty to let us know if any are moving west. Stay here tonight, lad.'

It was always like that. It wasn't that Con wanted to fight, but he felt lost and detached. Sometimes the lying talk with the puzzled, angry British troops seemed to infect his soul with the treason he mouthed to them. He acted so wholeheartedly that, as he talked to this officer or that, he *became* the 'loyal' small-minded clerk. He laughed fiercely sometimes, remembering, with bitterness, what he had said to some Englishman under the shadow of his own hills. For there was no doubt in his mind that he was on the right side. Many of the Irish fighters were fools – and worse; some were narrow-minded to an extent that appalled him; but they were all seeking a true thing. Under different forms it was seen by them, but it was a true thing.

And Con stayed on the outskirts in a misty region of words, hating the ambiguity, the dirtiness of his soft talk with the British. He was afraid of fighting, but he would have preferred it.

The summer of the blackest fighting came and in the first week of July the Column moved in on Cork City. Most came in as private individuals, somehow finding friends or relations to stay with in the west and south-west of the town. Headquarters, with most of the arms, was in a big deserted house near the small village of Waterfall, which lies in a hollow below its little chapel, about three miles south-west of the city. Something big had been planned, and Burke's Column was to take part. Only Burke himself had some idea of what was supposed to happen. Whatever it was it was taking a long time. Two weeks and still nothing, with Burke worrying about the discipline of his scattered men.

Con's father had died two months before, and the rent of the rooms in Cockpit Lane had lapsed, so at first Con didn't know where he would stay. He did not wish to ask any of his college friends, partly because he was poor and proud, and partly because he didn't want to mix the two worlds in which he lived: the IRA and the university. Surrounded by the atmosphere of one, the other always seemed as unreal as a dream, the legend of which, though strong in the heart, had nothing to do with living.

Stephanie Forde, the girl he was in love with, belonged to the world of the university. She loved him too and there were times when they seemed perfectly at one in their love. Yet he had not told her where he went when he disappeared from Cork for months on end. Her father, a well-to-do Cork doctor with the conservatism of his class, accepted him rather grudgingly as a possible future son-in-law, and her mother openly liked him. And it was at the Fordes' house in the Western Road that he finally stayed, when they discovered that he had nowhere to go.

'I suppose we couldn't let you starve in the street,' shouted Dr Forde, pompously humorous.

In the evenings, except on Friday when he cycled out to Waterfall by the back road, he helped Stephanie with work for her BA exam, which was coming soon. They would sit at the table in the dark Victorian dining-room surrounded by books while the evening grew quiet in the tree-lined Mardyke outside the window and the fading line of the hill above Sunday's Well marked its roads and houses with soft lights.

Stephanie was small and dark and unpredictable, and he loved her more all the time. She would work in great bursts, completely unlike his steady concentrated study. Sometimes he would watch her head bent stiffly over the page or her small hand charging up and down the lines with her green pen held in what seemed a hopelessly cramped position. Occasionally he answered the questions she flung at him. Sometimes he would talk to her of poetry or drama, and forget with his mind everything except the dancing of ideas and images, only his heart always remembering her presence. And often they would do no work at all, but make love and love talk in the summer dusk.

Inevitably, after a week of her company, he told her about his job with the IRA. To her it sounded like a brave and clever game, because he unconsciously acted the part of the daring spy to her as he told her. Her approval made him forget the reality of his IRA life, and while he was with her his petty spying seemed to him also a gallant adventure. Only when he reported to Burke at Waterfall on Friday evenings did the degrading reality weigh on him, and in consequence his admiration of his leader gave way to resentment and dislike. The practical details which constantly engaged Burke's attention seemed small and mean now.

'No signs of special activity, Con?'

'No, sir, nothing.'

'O'Malley and Lehane were arrested the other day for being out after curfew.They were drunk. Did you hear that?'

'No, sir.'

'Luckily they weren't carrying guns and they're all right. They swear they gave nothing away. That's all for today, Con; you can go now. Keep your eyes open, lad.'

'Yes, sir. Thanks, sir.'

Stephanie of course wanted to help him.

'Con, couldn't I do something to help? I'm sure I could find out things for you.'

Automatically he smiled the smile of the man who could find out anything by himself – the master spy.

'Ah, I know the ropes pretty well. There isn't anything you could do that I couldn't do just as well myself.'

'But I could go to dances that the British officers were at and get them to tell me things.'

'You could, my foot! Don't let me see or hear of you dancing with any bloody Englishmen.'

Besides his anger and anxiety there was a growing subconscious fear of letting the realities of his two worlds meet. This fear was his nightmare. It was a senseless but powerful terror.

It was a dry hot summer evening with an oppressive ceiling of low pearl-grey clouds. The small city was still with the stillness of lethargy. Fine dust lay on the pavements and on the leaves of trees unstirred by wind.

The Doctor was up at the Bon Secours Hospital. Mrs Forde was out. It was the girl's half-day. After tea Stephanie and Con, with the house to themselves, were trying to do some serious study.

Someone knocked authoritatively on the front door. 'I'll go,' said Con. He kissed her on the forehead and going out into the hall he opened the door. Facing him was the tall Major from whom Con had once extracted information in the course of a casual chat on a road near Kilmurry. Behind him a section of Tans. He looked hard at Con for a very long minute.

'Is Dr Forde in?'

'No. I'm terribly sorry, he won't be home for about two hours.' Con's voice rang loud and unreal in his own ears. 'Could I give him a message?'

'What is it, Con?' Stephanie came out of the dining-room. She stiffened when she saw the uniforms. Her face became stubborn and hostile. Con noticed with a distant part of his mind that she didn't even look pretty then. Hard and sharp.

'The Major is looking for your father,' said Con. He was conscious that he was smiling diffidently. The old habit.

The Major saluted Stephanie awkwardly. 'Miss Forde? I have been instructed to question your father about a man who died while he was attending to him. A wounded man. But, if your father is out, tomorrow will do. It's only routine.'

He talked in a rather dead voice, and as he did his eyes moved again to Con's face, puzzling his memory with familiarity. Con smiled vacantly at him.

'I think you'd better call tomorrow,' said Stephanie flatly.

'Right. Thank you, Miss Forde.' Then, slowly, to Con, 'I've seen you before. Can't place you though.'

'Probably around the city,' suggested Con. He tried to talk lightly, but the words seemed heavy and slow.

'I don't think so,' said the Major. 'I was stationed in Macroom until last week.' He paused, his eyes distant. Then suddenly he turned full on Con, shooting a question.

'Know Waterfall?'

The familiar name shocked Con. But this was his game. The Major was not certain of him. He was trying to snare him.

'Waterfall,' he said thoughtfully, 'yes, I believe I do, Major. A small place four miles or so from here. About south-west I should think. Why?' Push the questioning back at the bastard.

'Oh, nothing much. Just that we heard there were some rebels skulking there. South-west, four miles, you say?'

A poor cover-up, this seeking for information.

'Yes, I think so. One of the turns off the Bandon road if I remember rightly. Sorry to hear that those rascals are so close. I hope you deal with them, Major.'

'If they're there we'll get them all right. Thank you, Miss Forde. I'll call on your father tomorrow. Good evening.'

Con closed the door quietly and stood for a minute looking at nothing, feeling Stephanie's anger in the dark hall.

'Come into the dining-room before you talk,' he said.

Beside the table she turned on him in anger. He was glad it was anger and not scorn with a cold hard face.

'Con, how could you! Sucking up to that man, with a soft voice and your talk of "rebels." And telling where Waterfall was!'

Con felt that she was very, very far away. Out of touch. He fought with this feeling, trying to be aware of her view.

'To answer you categorically,' he said stiffly. 'First, as I've explained before, they've got to be lulled by "loyalty"–'

'Yes,' she said, 'but not like *that*!'

He felt like asking her how it was to be done then, but he knew it would be no good so he went on:

'Second, I had met him before and got information out of him, and he nearly remembered me. Thirdly, he knew where Waterfall was. He was testing me. Our company HQ is, or was, there. Somebody split on us.'

'Your headquarters is there?' Her voice was high.

'Well, anyway, it was, but I expect the British are either on their way there now or else they raided it last night. It's not far. It's the place I go to report on Fridays.' He sat down heavily.

'But, Con,' said Stephanie, looking at him in angry astonishment, 'surely you're going to do something. Surely you're not just going to sit there!'

A great weariness came over Con. He seemed anchored forever to the hard chair and the soft carpet, in the dark room with her anger and ignorance. But he forced himself to speak.

'Arra, do what, girl?' he said. 'Even if they're not there yet, they'll have the place surrounded and the roads watched. It's no good, I'm telling you.'

'So you're not going to try and warn them?'

'No,' he said, 'I'm not that foolish.'

She gave him a dark look and left the room. He heard her go upstairs and then come down to the hall again. The coat stand rocked on the loose board. He went out uneasily. She was standing in the hall with her coat on.

'Where do you think you're going?' he asked.

'To Waterfall, of course. If you're frightened to go I must then. I know my duty.'

'Ah, for God's sake, Stephanie, don't be stupid,' he said despairingly. 'If there was a dog's chance I'd go myself.' He took hold of her arm, but she jerked it away, flicking her dark hair across her cheek as she did.

'I'm going.'

He stared at her white face and saw she meant it. His hands felt heavy with shame and anger. Suddenly he shrugged.

'Take off your coat, Stephanie, I'll go myself on the bike.'

'You won't just pretend to go?'

'I swear to God I'll go.'

'Ah, I knew you'd see I was right,' she said joyfully. 'We have to try and save them. But you'll be careful, won't you, Con? You'll go by the back lanes?'

He choked back bitter words.

'I'll be fine,' he said in a still voice. 'And now don't say any more. I'll go now and it will be dark when I get there.'

She might as well have shot me now, he thought.

Yet there was a certain liberation in action. He went up to his room and put on a raincoat. Into the pocket he pushed his revolver. He tucked his trouser ends in his socks, went to the lavatory, and then came downstairs. Stephanie was waiting in the hall. She was rather pale and she gave him a soft fierce kiss.

He held her shoulders and looked at her. His feelings were a confusion of irritation and despairing sadness.

'I love you,' he said, kissed her between the eyes, and went out the back way to get his bike.

It was a quarter to eight. Curfew began at the hour. That gave him plenty of time to get out of the city if he wasn't stopped. He would go out the Lee Road and come back carefully on Waterfall from the north-west, using the side roads.

By the time the city was behind him he had almost forgotten the risk he was running. On his left the Lee ran softly through quiet evening fields where cattle moved as if in sleep under the grey sky. Beyond the river, beyond the fields, there were low hills half-covered with trees. On the right the wooded slope of Mount Desert rose steeply. It was very quiet.

After a while the road climbed sidling up the hill into the pillared green of a beech wood. Here Con waited for half an hour. He did not want to get to Waterfall before dark. He sat without thought in the stillness of the trees watching the river grow faintly luminous in the gathering twilight of the valley.

Then he moved on, going with more speed and care. It was nearly dark when he came over the top of the little hill opposite the house. He stopped and watched. The house was quiet among its trees; no light in any window; not a sound. After ten minutes he went down the road and left his bicycle in a field. Then he walked up the dark lane to the gate. Still nothing. Either he was in time to warn Burke or else the Commandant had already been given the word and was gone.

In the gloom he saw that the windows of the front room which Burke used were still shuttered and that the front door stood as usual a little ajar. He slipped into the hall. A faint crack of candle-light showed under the door of Burke's room. In time, he thought, and opening the door he walked in.

A British captain was sitting behind the table with the candle-light on his tired young face; behind him two soldiers covered Con with their rifles.

'Put your hands up,' said the Captain quietly.

He obeyed, his mind blank with surprise.

'Search him,' said the Captain.

A big bull of a man moved out of the shadows and frisked Con's pockets with heavy red hands. He grunted as he felt the revolver, pulled it out, broke it and put it on the table.

'I was told that you might come,' said the Captain in a hard voice. 'You are accused of spying for the rebels.' He half turned in his chair and shouted in a petulant voice: 'Mr Gregg! Mr Gregg!'

A tall subaltern with a round pale face blundered through the door from the inner room, and obeying a sign from the Captain sat down at the table beside him.

'Well?' said the Captain to Con. 'Have you anything to say?'

Con felt the futility of it; but he fumbled automatically for words. Just as he opened his mouth to speak the Captain said rapidly: 'The rebels who were hiding here got away before we arrived. You probably know where they are. Perhaps you know of others too.' His voice grew slower, wearily emphatic. 'If you give us any information leading to the finding of these men, especially their leaders, I have been instructed to tell you that you stand a good chance of getting off with a prison sentence.' His drawn face looked curiously at Con.

By now Con had got over the shock of being caught, but fear stirred under his surface thoughts. Burke and the men had got away. Someone had talked. He felt deserted. His comrades seemed remote. He became aware of a great useless longing for peace, for Stephanie, for his books. Burke and Ireland could go to hell. He knew enough to get himself free. And not a soul need know. He raised his heavy eyes. What he saw was the Captain's face full of a tired bullying eagerness. Stupid, and confident that he could get what he wanted. A terrible anger came up in Con's chest: anger at this pushing stupidity and bullying confidence in the small tired man at the table.

'You can all go to hell,' he said in a high shaking voice. And then lower and firmer, 'You can all go to hell.'

There was a short silence.

'Very well,' said the Captain in an expressionless voice. 'Gregg, detail a section. You will be in charge, Sergeant-Major.'

The moon-faced Lieutenant went through into the next room. A soft voice in there said, 'Draw cards.'

'You're sure you've nothing to tell us?' said the Captain in the same meaningless voice.

Con said nothing. He stared at the swaying bulk of one of the soldiers behind the table. He should try to pray. He crossed himself quickly and clumsily, his eyes moving to the candle on the table. He tried to think of Stephanie but all he could remember was a rather ugly bracelet that she often wore.

The pale face of the Captain moved near the brown face of the Sergeant-Major with low earnest words. Feet scraped on the floor as six soldiers, indistinct in the shadows, filed into the room.

'Right, Sergeant-Major.'

'Right, sir.'

Their bodies moved around him. He turned with them and walked out into the dark. The door closed.

The young Captain still sat at the table looking at his hands. Voices moved in the next room.

After about three minutes the rifles shattered the night outside. No pistol shot.

The Sergeant-Major came in quietly.

'Sir.'

'We stay here tonight. Post fresh sentries and see that the men get food and perhaps some tea. I don't want any.'

'Yes, sir.' The voice had a note of solicitude which irritated the young Captain. 'Good night, sir.'

The Captain did not answer.

And after the Lieutenant had turned in, he still sat with his elbows on the scratched boards of the table, staring at the white candle flame, on the black twist of the wick. So clear. So bright.

The Sniper

LIAM O'FLAHERTY 1930

The end of the Irish War of Independence in 1921, resulting in the Irish Free State, should have brought peace but instead it brought civil war. The Free Staters accepted the Peace Treaty with Britain which left six counties in the north as part of the UK, as is still the case. The Republicans wanted all of the 32 counties to be one Republic. The war commenced immediately after British troops withdrew from the new Free State. This story is set in the centre of Dublin but feelings were passionate all over Ireland and families were divided, often with tragic results as this story shows.

The long June evening faded into night. Dublin lay in darkness; only the faint light of a pale moon shone through thin clouds, over the streets and the dark waters of the River Liffey. Around the Four Courts, where fighting was constant, the heavy guns roared. Here and there, through the city, machine-guns and rifles broke the silence of the night, like dogs barking on lonely farms. Irishmen were fighting Irishmen: civil war.

On a roof-top near O'Connell Bridge, a Republican sniper lay watching. Beside him lay his rifle and over his shoulders hung a pair of field-glasses. His face was the face of a student – thin and prepared for sacrifice, but his eyes shone with the cold light of the fanatic. They were deep and thoughtful, the eyes of a man who is used to looking at death.

He was eating a sandwich hungrily. He had eaten nothing since morning. He had been too excited to eat. He finished the sandwich and, taking a flask of whiskey from his pocket, he had a quick drink. Then he returned the flask to his pocket. He paused for a moment, considering whether he should risk a smoke. It was dangerous. The flash might be seen in the darkness and there were enemies watching. He decided to take the risk. Placing a cigarette between his lips, he struck a match, drew some smoke into his lungs quickly and put out the light.

Almost immediately a bullet flattened itself against the parapet of the roof. The sniper drew again quickly on his cigarette and put it out; then he swore softly and crawled away to the left.

Cautiously he raised himself and looked over the parapet. There was a flash and a bullet shot over his head. He dropped immediately. He had seen the flash. It came from the opposite side of the street.

He rolled across the roof to a chimney in the rear and slowly pulled himself up on his feet behind it until his eyes were level with the top of the parapet. There was nothing to be seen – just the faint outline of the opposite housetop against the blue sky. His enemy was under cover.

Just then an armoured car came across the bridge and advanced slowly up the street. It stopped on the opposite side of the street fifty yards ahead. The sniper could hear the dull noise of the motor, like an animal breathing. His heart beat faster. It was an enemy car. He wanted to shoot but he knew it was useless. His bullets would never cut through the steel that covered the grey metal beast.

Then round the corner of a side street came an old woman, her head covered by an old shawl. She began to talk to the man in the turret of the car. She was pointing to the roof where the sniper lay. An informer.

The turret opened. A man's head and shoulders appeared, looking towards the sniper. The sniper raised his rifle and shot. The head fell heavily on the turret wall. The woman made a run towards the side street. The sniper shot again. The woman twisted rapidly round and fell with a long sharp cry into the gutter.

Suddenly from the opposite roof a shot sounded sharply and the sniper swore and dropped his rifle. The rifle fell noisily to the roof. The sniper thought the noise would wake the dead. He bent down to pick the rifle up. He couldn't lift it. His forearm was dead. 'Christ,' he said in a low voice, 'I'm hit.'

Dropping flat on the roof, he crawled back to the parapet. With his left hand he felt the wounded right forearm. Blood was beginning to appear through the sleeve of his coat. There was no pain – just a deadened feeling as if the arm had been cut off.

Quickly he drew his knife from his pocket, opened it on the stone-work of the parapet and tore open the sleeve. There was a small hole where the bullet had entered. On the other side there was no hole. The bullet had stuck in the bone. It must have broken it. He bent the arm below the wound. The arm bent back easily. He ground his teeth to overcome the pain.

Then, taking out his field-dressing, he tore open the packet with his knife. He broke the neck of the iodine bottle and let the bitter liquid fall drop by drop into the wound. His whole body shook with the sharp pain of it. He placed the cotton wool over the wound and wrapped a bandage over it. He tied the end with his teeth.

Then he lay still against the parapet and, closing his eyes, he made an effort of will to overcome the pain.

In the street beneath, all was still. The armoured car had retired speedily over the bridge, with the machine-gunner's head hanging lifeless over the turret. The dead body of the woman lay still in the gutter.

The sniper lay for a long time nursing his wounded arm and planning escape. When morning came, he must not be found wounded on the roof. The enemy on the opposite roof was covering his escape. He must kill that enemy and he could not use his rifle. He had only a revolver to kill him with. Then he thought of a plan.

Taking off his cap, he placed it over the end of his rifle. Then he pushed the rifle slowly upwards over the parapet until the cap could be seen from the opposite side of the street. Almost immediately a shot sounded and a bullet went right through the centre of the cap. The sniper then let the rifle hang forward and downward. The cap slipped down into the street. Then, catching the rifle in the middle, the sniper dropped his left hand over the roof and let it hang, lifelessly. After a few moments he let the rifle drop to the street. Then he sank to the roof, dragging his hand with him.

Crawling quickly to the left, he looked up at the corner of the opposite roof. His trick had succeeded. The other sniper, seeing the cap and rifle fall, thought that he had killed his man. He was now standing in front of a row of chimneys looking across, with his head clearly outlined against the western sky.

The Republican sniper smiled and lifted his revolver above the edge of the parapet. The distance was about fifty yards – a hard shot in the poor light – and the pain in his right arm was hurting him like a thousand devils. He took a steady aim. His hand was almost shaking with eagerness. Pressing his lips together, he breathed in deeply through his nose and shot. He was almost deafened with the noise and his arm shook with the recoil.

Then, when the smoke cleared, he looked carefully across and gave out a cry of joy. His enemy had been hit. He was rolling from side to side over the parapet in his death agony. He struggled to stay on his feet but he was slowly falling forward as if in a dream. The rifle fell from his hand, hit the parapet, fell over, bounded off the pole of a barber's shop beneath and then dropped noisily on to the road.

Then the dying man on the roof bent double and fell forward. The body turned over and over in space and hit the ground with a dull thud. Then it lay still.

The sniper looked at his enemy falling and his body shook once. The fierce love of battle died in him. He became filled with sadness at what he had done. The sweat stood out in small round drops on his forehead. Weakened by his wound and the long summer day of going without food and watching on the roof, he felt sickened at the sight of the torn and broken mass of his dead enemy. His teeth chattered. He began to talk rubbish to himself, cursing the war, cursing himself, cursing everybody.

He looked at the smoking revolver in his hand and with a curse he threw it hard to the roof, at his feet. The force of the fall made the revolver go off and the bullet shot close past the sniper's head. He was frightened back to his senses by the shock. His nerves steadied. The cloud of fear lifted from his mind and he laughed.

Drawing the whiskey flask from his pocket, he took one long drink and emptied it. He felt less cautious under the influence of the drink. He decided to leave the roof and look for his company commander so that he could report what had happened. Everywhere around was quiet. There was not much danger in going through the streets. He picked up his revolver and put it in his pocket. Then he crawled down through the sky-light to the house underneath.

When the sniper reached street level, he felt a sudden curiosity as to the identity of the enemy sniper whom he had killed. He decided that he could shoot well, whoever he was. He wondered if he knew him. Perhaps he had been in his own company before the army had split into two. He decided to take a chance and go over to have a look at him. He looked carefully around the corner into O'Connell Street. In the upper part of the street was heavy gunfire, but around here all was quiet.

The sniper ran across the street. A machine-gun tore up the ground around him with a shower of bullets, but he escaped. He threw himself face downwards beside the dead body. The machine-gun stopped.

Then the sniper turned over the body and looked into his brother's face.

The Wall Reader

FIONA BARR 1979

Belfast is the biggest city in Northern Ireland, a town where peace and politically inspired violence can co-exist. Most people seek to lead ordinary lives and succeed as they go to work, to school – or take their baby for an afternoon stroll in the local park. Sometimes, however, the atmosphere of fear and suspicion forces the innocent (or thoughtless?) out of their own city.

'Shall only our rivers run free?' The question jumped out from the cobbled wall in huge white letters, as The People's taxi swung round the corner at Beechmount. 'Looks like paint is running freely enough down here,' she thought to herself, as other slogans glided past in rapid succession. Reading Belfast's grim graffiti had become an entertaining hobby for her, and she often wondered, was it in the dead of night that groups of boys huddled round a paint tin daubing walls and gables with tired political slogans and clichés? Did anyone ever see them? Was the guilty brush ever found? The brush is mightier than the bomb, she declared inwardly, as she thought of how celebrated among journalists some lines had become. 'Is there a life before death?' Well, no one had answered that one yet, at least not in this city.

The shapes of Belfast crowded in on her as the taxi rattled over the ramps outside the fortressed police barracks. Dilapidated houses, bricked-up terraces. Rosy-cheeked soldiers, barely out of school, and quivering with high-pitched fear. She thought of the thick-lipped youth who came to hijack the car, making his point by showing his revolver under his anorak, and of the others, jigging and taunting every July, almost sexual in their arrogance and hatred. Meanwhile, passengers climbed in and out at various points along the road, manoeuvring between legs, bags of shopping and umbrellas. The taxi swerved blindly into the road. No Highway Code here. As the woman's stop approached, the taxi swung up to the pavement, and she stepped out.

She thought of how she read walls – like tea-cups, she smiled to herself. Pushing her baby in the pram to the supermarket, she had to pass under a motorway bridge that was peppered with lines, some in irregular lettering with the paint dribbling down the concrete, others written with felt-tip pen in

All the Queen's Horses . . . by Dermot Seymour

a minute secretive hand. A whole range of human emotions splayed itself with persistent anarchy on the walls. 'One could do worse than be a reader of walls,' she thought, twisting Frost's words. Instead, though, the pram was rushed past the intriguing mural with much gusto. Respectable housewives don't read walls!

The 'Troubles', as they were euphemistically named, remained for this couple as a remote, vaguely irritating wart on their life. They were simply ordinary (she often groaned at the oppressive banality of the word), middle class, and hoping the baby would marry a doctor, thereby raising them in their autumn days to the select legions of the upper class. Each day their lives followed the same routine – no harm in that sordid little detail, she thought. It helps structure one's existence. He went to the office, she fed the baby, washed the rapidly growing mound of nappies, prepared the dinner and looked forward to the afternoon walk. She had convinced herself she was happy with her lot, and yet felt disappointed at the pangs of jealousy endured on hearing of a friend's glamorous job or another's academic and erudite husband. If only someone noticed her from time to time, or even wrote her name on a wall declaring her existence worthwhile: 'A fine mind' or 'I was once her lover.' That way, at least, she would have evidence she was having impact on others. As it was, she was perpetually bombarded with it. Marital successes, even marital failures evoked a response from her. All one-way traffic.

That afternoon she dressed the baby and started out for her walk. 'Fantasy time' her husband called it. 'Wall-reading time' she knew it to be. On this occasion, however, she decided to avoid those concrete temptations and, instead, visit the park. Out along the main road she trundled, pushing the pram, pausing to gaze into the hardware store's window, hearing the whine of the Saracen as it thundered by, waking the baby and making her feel uneasy. A foot patrol of soldiers strolled past, their rifles, lethal even in the brittle sunlight of this March day, lounged lovingly and relaxed in the arms of their men. One soldier stood nonchalantly, almost impertinent, against a corrugated railing and stared at her. She always blushed on passing troops.

The park is ugly, stark and hostile. Even in summer, when courting couples seek out secluded spots like mating cats, they reject Musgrave. There are a few trees, clustered together, standing like skeletons, ashamed of their nakedness. The rest is grass, a green wasteland speckled with puddles of gulls squawking over a worm patch. The park is bordered by a hospital with a

military wing which is guarded by an army billet. The beauty of the place – it
has only this – is its silence.

The hill up to the park bench was not the precipice it seemed, but the baby
and the pram were heavy. Antenatal self-indulgence had taken its toll – her
midriff was now most definitely a bulge. With one final push, pram, baby and
mother reached the green wooden seat, and came to rest. The baby slept
soundly with the soother touching her velvet pink cheeks, hand on pillow, a
picture of purity. The woman heard a coughing noise coming from the nearby
gun turret, and managed to see the tip of a rifle and a face peering out from the
darkness. Smells of cabbage and burnt potatoes wafted over from behind the
slanting sheets of protective steel.

'Is that your baby?' an English voice called out. She could barely see the face
belonging to the voice. She replied yes, and smiled. The situation reminded her
of the confessional. Dark and supposedly anonymous, 'Is that you, my child?'
She knew the priest personally. Did he identify her sins with his 'Good
morning, Mary,' and think to himself, 'and I know what you were up to last
night!' She blushed at the secrets given away during the ceremony. Yes, she
nervously answered again, it was her baby, a little girl. First-time mothers
rarely resist the temptation to talk about their offspring. Forgetting her initial
shyness, she told the voice of when the baby was born, the early problems of
all-night crying, now teething, how she could crawl backwards and gurgle.

The voice responded. It too had a son, a few months older than her child,
away in Germany at the army base at Munster. Factory pipes, chimney tops,
church spires, domes all listened impassively to the Englishman's declaration
of paternal love. The scene was strange, for although Belfast's sterile
geography slipped into classical forms with dusk and heavy rain-clouds, the
voice and the woman knew the folly of such innocent communication. They
politely finished their conversation, said goodbye, and the woman pushed her
pram homewards. The voice remained in the turret, watchful and anxious.
Home she went, past vanloads of workers leering out at the pavement, past
the uneasy presence of foot patrols, past the church. 'Let us give each other
the sign of peace,' they said at Mass. The only sign Belfast knew was two
fingers pointing towards Heaven. Life was self-contained, the couple often
declared, just like flats. No need to go outside.

She did go outside, however. Each week the voice and the woman learned
more of each other. No physical contact was needed, no face-to-face
encounter to judge reaction, no touching to confirm amity, no threat of

dangerous intimacy. It was a meeting of minds, as she explained later to her husband, a new opinion, a common bond, an opening of vistas. He disclosed his ambitions to become a pilot, watching the land, fields and horizons spread out beneath him – a patchwork quilt of dappled colours and textures. She wanted to be remembered by writing on walls, about them that is, a world-shattering thesis on their psychological complexities, their essential truths, their witticisms and intellectual genius. And all this time the city's skyline and distant buildings watched and listened.

It was April now. More slogans had appeared, white and dripping, on the city walls. 'Brits out. Peace in.' A simple equation for the writer. 'Loose talk claims lives,' another shouted menacingly. The messages, the woman decided, had acquired a more ominous tone. The baby had grown and could sit up without support. New political solutions had been proposed and rejected, inter-paramilitary feuding had broken out and subsided, four soldiers and two policemen had been blown to smithereens in separate incidents, and a building a day had been bombed by the Provos. It had been a fairly normal month by Belfast's standards. The level of violence was no more or less acceptable than at other times.

One day – it was, perhaps, the last day in April – her husband returned home panting and trembling a little. He asked had she been to the park, and she replied she had. Taking her by the hand, he led her to the wall on the left of their driveway. She felt her heart sink and thud against her. She felt her face redden. Her mouth was suddenly dry. She could not speak. In huge angry letters the message spat itself out,

'TOUT'

The four-letter word covered the whole wall. It clanged in her brain, its venom rushed through her body. Suspicion was enough to condemn. The job itself was not well done, she had seen better. The letters were uneven, paint splattered down from the cross T, the U looked a misshapen O. The workmanship was poor, the impact perfect.

Her husband led her back into the kitchen. The baby was crying loudly in the living-room but the woman did not seem to hear. Like sleepwalkers, they sat down on the settee. The woman began to sob. Her shoulders heaved in bursts as she gasped hysterically. Her husband took her in his arms gently and tried to make her sorrow his. Already he shared her fear.

'What did you talk about? Did you not realise how dangerous it was? We must leave.' He spoke quickly, making plans. Selling the house and car, finding a job in London or Dublin, far away from Belfast, mortgages, removals, savings, the tawdry affairs of normal living stunned her, making her more confused. 'I told him nothing,' she sobbed, 'what could I tell? We talked about life, everything, but not about here.' She trembled, trying to control herself. 'We just chatted about reading walls, families, anything at all. Oh Sean, it was as innocent as that. A meeting of minds we called it, for it was little else.'

She looked into her husband's face and saw he did not fully understand. There was a hint of jealousy, of resentment at not being part of their communication. Her hands fell on her lap, resting in resignation. What was the point of explanation? She lifted her baby from the floor. Pressing the tiny face and body to her breast, she felt all her hopes and desires for a better life become one with the child's struggle for freedom. The child's hands wandered over her face, their eyes met. At once that moment of maternal and filial love eclipsed her fear, gave her the impetus to escape.

For nine months she had been unable to accept the reality of her condition. Absurd, for the massive bump daily shifted position and thumped against her. When her daughter was born, she had been overwhelmed by love for her and amazed at her own ability to give life. By nature she was a dreamy person, given to moments of fancy. She wondered at her competence in fulfilling the role of mother. Could it be measured? This time she knew it could. She really did not care if they maimed her or even murdered her. She did care about her daughter. She was her touchstone, her anchor to virtue. Not for her child a legacy of fear, revulsion or hatred. With the few hours' respite the painters had left between judgement and sentence she determined to leave Belfast's walls behind.

The next few nights were spent in troubled, restless sleep. The message remained on the wall outside. The neighbours pretended not to notice and refused to discuss the matter. She and the baby remained indoors despite the refreshing May breezes and blue skies. Her husband had given in his notice at the office, for health reasons, he suggested to his colleagues. An aunt had been contacted in Dublin. The couple did not answer knocks at the door. They carefully examined the shape and size of mail delivered and always paused when they answered the telephone.

The mini-van was to call at eleven on Monday night, when it would be dark enough to park, and pack their belongings and themselves without too much suspicion being aroused. The firm had been very understanding when the nature of their work had been explained. They were Protestant so there was no conflict of loyalties involved in the exercise. They agreed to drive them to Dublin at extra cost, changing drivers at Newry on the way down.

Monday finally arrived. The couple nervously laughed about how smoothly everything had gone. Privately, they each expected something to go wrong. The baby was fed, and played with, the radio listened to and the clock watched. They listened to the news at nine. Huddled together in their anxiety, they kept vigil in the darkening room. Rain had begun to pour from black thunderclouds. Everywhere it was quiet and still. Hushed and cold they waited. Ten o'clock, and it was now dark. A blustery wind had risen, making the lattice separation next door bang and clatter. At ten to eleven, her husband went into the sitting-room to watch for the mini-van. His footsteps clamped noisily on the floorboards as he paced back and forth. The baby slept.

A black shape glided slowly up the street and backed into the driveway. It was eleven. The van had arrived. Her husband asked to see their identification and then they began to load up the couple's belongings. Settee, chairs, television, washing machine – all were dumped hastily, it was no time to worry about breakages. She stood holding the sleeping baby in the living-room as the men worked anxiously between van and house. The scene was so unreal, the circumstances absolutely incredible. She thought, 'What have I done?' Recollections of her naïvety, her insensibility to historical fact and political climate were stupefying. She had seen women who had been tarred and feathered, heard of people who had been shot in the head, boys who had been knee-capped, all for suspected fraternising with troops. The catalogue of violence spilled out before her as she realised the gravity and possible repercussions of her alleged misdemeanour.

A voice called her, 'Mary, come on now. We have to go. Don't worry, we're all together.' Her husband led her to the locked and waiting van. Handing the baby to him, she climbed up beside the driver, took back the baby as her husband sat down beside her and waited for the engine to start. The van slowly manoeuvred out onto the street and down the main road. They felt more cheerful now, a little like refugees seeking safety and freedom not too far away. As they approached the motorway bridge, two figures with something clutched in their hands stood side by side in the darkness. She closed her eyes tightly, expecting bursts of gunfire. The van shot past. Relieved, she asked her husband what they were doing at this time of night. 'Writing slogans on the wall,' he replied.

The furtiveness of the painters seemed ludicrous and petty as she recalled the heroic and literary characteristics with which she had endowed them. What did they matter? The travellers sat in silence as the van sped past the city suburbs, the glare of police and army barracks, on out and further out into the countryside. Past sleeping villages and silent fields, past whitewashed farmhouses and barking dogs. On to Newry where they said goodbye to their driver as the new one stepped in. Far along the coast with Rostrevor's twinkling lights opposite the bay down to the Border check and a drowsy soldier waving them through. Out of the North, safe, relieved and heading for Dublin.

Some days later in Belfast the neighbours discovered the house vacant, the people next door received a letter and a cheque from Dublin. Remarks about the peculiar couple were made over hedges and cups of coffee. The message on the wall was painted over by the couple who had bought the house when it went up for sale. They too were ordinary people, living a self-contained life, worrying over finance and babies, promotion and local gossip. He too had an office job, but his wife was merely a housekeeper for him. She was sensible, down-to-earth, and not in the least inclined to wall-reading.

Oranges from Spain

DAVID PARK 1988

The man who tells this story recalls taking a school-holiday job in a greengrocer's shop in Belfast. In his adolescent superiority he saw his boss as a tight-fisted and narrow-minded man but he came to discover hidden dimensions to Gerry Breen's life, of pain and kindness and dreams. Such knowledge dawned slowly but the bitter shock of loss, and lost opportunity for friendship, would remain with the boy throughout his adult life.

It's not a fruit shop any more. Afterwards, his wife sold it and someone opened up a fast-food business. You wouldn't recognise it now – it's all flashing neon, girls in identical uniforms and the type of food that has no taste. Even Gerry Breen wouldn't recognise it. Either consciously or unconsciously, I don't seem to pass that way very often, but when I do I always stop and look at it. The neon brightness burns the senses and sears the memories like a wound being cauterised; but then it all comes back and out flows a flood of memory that nothing can stem.

I was sixteen years old and very young when I went to work for Mr Breen in his fruit shop. It was that summer when it seemed to rain every day and a good day stood out like something special. I got the job through patronage. My father and Gerry Breen went back a long way – that always struck me as strange, because they were so unalike as men. Apparently, they were both born in the same street and grew up together, and even when my father's career as a solicitor took him upmarket, they still got together occasionally. My father collected an order of fruit every Friday night on his way home from work, and as children we always talked about 'Gerry Breen's apples'. It's funny the things you remember, and I can recall very clearly my mother and father having an argument about it one day. She wanted to start getting fruit from the supermarket for some reason, but my father wouldn't hear of it. He got quite agitated about it and almost ended up shouting, which was very unlike him. Maybe he acted out of loyalty, or maybe he owed him some kind of favour, but whatever the reason, the arrangement continued.

If his name is mentioned now they never do it in front of me. It's almost as if he never existed. At first it angered me – it was almost as if they thought I would disintegrate at its sound – but gradually I came to be grateful for it. I didn't even go to the funeral, and from that moment it was obvious my family sought to draw a curtain over the whole event. My mother had taken me away for a week's holiday. We stayed with one of her sisters who lives in Donegal, and I've never had a more miserable time. Inevitably, it rained every day and there was nothing to do but mope around and remember, trapped in a house full of women, where the only sounds were the clink of china cups and the click of knitting needles. It was then the dreams started. The intervening years have lessened their frequency but not their horror. When I woke up screaming for about the tenth time, they took me to a special doctor who reassured them with all the usual platitudes – I'd grow out of it, time was a great healer, and so on. In one sense I did grow out of it – I stopped telling anyone about the nightmares and kept them strictly private. They don't come very often now, but when they do only my wife knows. Sometimes she cradles me in her arms like a child until I fall asleep again.

I hadn't even really wanted a job in the first place. It was all my father's idea. He remembered the long weeks of boredom I had complained about the summer before and probably the nuisance I had been as I lazed about the house. I walked right into his trap. He knew I'd been working up to ask if I could have a motorbike for my next birthday. The signs weren't good, and my mother's instinctive caution would have been as difficult a barrier to surmount as the expense, so it came as a surprise when my father casually enquired if I'd be interested in starting to save for one. I took the bait, and before I knew what was happening, I'd been fixed up with a summer job, working in Gerry Breen's fruit shop.

I didn't like the man much at first. He was rough and ready and he would've walked ten miles on his knees to save a penny. I don't think he liked me much either. The first day he saw me he looked me up and down with unconcealed disappointment, with the expression of someone who'd just bought a horse that wasn't strong enough to do the work he had envisaged for it. He stopped short of feeling my arm muscles, but passed some comment about me needing to fill out a bit. Although he wasn't tall himself, he was squat and had a kind of stocky strength about him that carried him through every physical situation. You knew that when he put his shoulder to the wheel, the chances were the wheel would spin. He wore this green coat as if it was some sort of uniform, and I never saw him in the shop without it. It was shiny at the elbows and collar, but it always looked clean. He had sandy-coloured hair that was slicked back and oiled down in a style that suggested he had once had an affinity with the Teddy boys. The first time I met him I noticed his hands, which were flat and square, and his chisel-shaped fingers. He had this little red pen-knife, and at regular intervals he used it to clean them. The other habit he had was a continual hitching-up of his trousers, even though there was no apparent prospect of them falling down. He was a man who seemed to be in perpetual motion. Even when he was standing talking to someone, there was always some part of him that was moving, whether it was transferring his pencil from one ear to the other, or hoisting up the trousers. It was as if there was a kind of mechanism inside him. Sometimes I saw him shuffle his feet through three hundred and sixty degrees like some kind of clockwork toy. For him sitting still would have been like wearing a strait-jacket, and I don't think any chair, no matter how comfortable, ever held him for more than a few minutes.

On my first morning, after his initial disappointment had worn off and he had obviously resolved to make the best of a bad job, he handed me a green coat, similar to his own but even older. It had a musty smell about it that suggested it had been hanging in a dark cupboard for some considerable time, and although I took it home that first weekend for my mother to wash, I don't think the smell ever left it. The sleeves were too long, so all summer I wore it with the cuffs turned up. My first job was chopping sticks. As well as fruit and vegetables, he sold various other things, including bundles of firewood. Out in the back yard was a mountain of wood, mostly old fruit boxes, and for the rest of that morning I chopped them into sticks and put them in polythene bags. At regular intervals he came out to supervise the work and caution me with monotonous regularity to be careful with the hatchet. It was obvious I wasn't doing it to his satisfaction; his dissatisfaction was communicated by a narrowing of his eyes and a snakelike hiss. As far as I was concerned, there weren't too many ways you could chop sticks, but I was wrong. Unable to restrain his frustration any longer, he took the hatchet and proceeded to instruct me in the correct technique. This involved gently inserting it into the end of the piece of wood and then tapping the other end lightly on the ground so that it split gently along the grain. When he was assured I had mastered the method, he watched critically over my first efforts.

'Too thick, son, too thick. Did your da never teach you how to chop sticks?'

It was only when I had produced a series of the thinnest slivers that he seemed content. I suppose it meant he got more bundles of firewood, but you wouldn't have got much of a fire out of them. It made me feel guilty somehow, like I was an accessory to his stinginess. 'Did your da never teach you how to?' was a phrase I heard repeatedly that summer, and it inevitably prefaced a period of instruction in the correct technique and subsequent supervision.

The rest of my time that first morning was divided between sweeping up and humping bags of spuds from the yard into the store-room. No matter how often I brushed that shop floor, it always seemed to need to be done again. I must have filled a whole dump with cauliflower leaves, and I never stopped hating that smell. Perhaps, if I'm honest, I felt the job was a little beneath me. By the time the day was over, my back was aching and I was still trying to extract splinters from my hands. The prospect of a summer spent working like that filled me with despondency, and the attraction of a motorbike lost some of its appeal. I thought of telling my father I didn't want to go back, but was stopped by the knowledge that I would have to listen to eternal speeches about how soft young people were, and how they wanted everything on a plate. That I didn't need, and so I resolved to grit my teeth and stick it out.

The shop was situated at the bottom of the Antrim Road, and while it wasn't that big, every bit of space was used, either for display or storage. It started outside on the pavement where each morning, after carrying out wooden trestles and resting planks on them, we set out trays of fruit, carefully arranged and hand-picked, designed to attract and entice the passer-by. Above all this stretched a green canvas canopy which was supported by ancient iron stanchions, black with age. When it rained it would drip on to the front displays of fruit and so all that summer I had to carry them in and out of the shop. Inside was a long counter with old-fashioned scales and a till that rang as loudly as church bells. Under the counter were paper bags of every size, miles of string, metal hooks, bamboo canes, withered yellow rubber gloves, weights, elastic bands and a paraphernalia of utensils of unfathomable purpose. On the wall behind the counter was an assortment of glass-fronted shelving, sagging under the weight of fruit and vegetables. Above head height, the walls were covered in advertising posters that had obviously arrived free with consignments of fruit and looked like they had been there since the shop opened. On the customer side was more shelving and below it a clutter of wooden and cardboard boxes that seemed designed to ladder tights or catch the wheels of shopping trolleys. If there was any kind of logical system in the layout, I never managed to work it out. I got the impression it had evolved into a sprawling disorder and that so long as everything was close at hand, the owner saw no reason to change it.

In the back of the shop was a store-room where among merchandise and debris stood a wooden table, two chairs, a gas cooker and a sink. The only other room was a small washroom. Beyond this was a small cobbled yard, enclosed by a brick wall topped with broken glass. Over everything hung the sweet, ripe smell of a fruit shop, but in Mr Breen's shop it was mixed with a mildewed mustiness, a strange hybrid that stayed in my senses long after I had left the scene.

I worked my butt off that first day and it was obvious he intended getting value for money out of me. Maybe my father had told him it was what I needed – I don't know. It was nearly time to close and the shop was empty. He was working out some calculations on the back of a brown paper bag and I was moving fruit into the store-room, when he glanced up at me with a kind of puzzled look, as if he was trying to work out what I was thinking.

'Sure, son, it's money for old rope. Isn't that right?'

I gave a non-committal nod of my head and kept on working. Then he told me I could go, and I could tell he was wondering whether he would see me the next day. Returning to his calculations again, he licked the stub of the pencil he was using and hitched up his trousers. I said goodbye and just as I was going out the door he called me back.

'Do you want to know something, son?'

I looked at him, unsure of what response he expected. Then, signalling me closer, he whispered loudly, 'My best friends are bananas.' I forced a smile at his joke, then walked out into the street and took a deep breath of fresh air.

The fruit shop did steady business. Most of the trade came from the housewives who lived in the neighbourhood, but there was also a regular source of custom from people who arrived outside the shop in cars, and by their appearance didn't live locally – the type who bought garlic. He knew them all by name and sometimes even had their order already made up, always making a fuss over them and getting me to carry it out to their car. They were obviously long-standing customers, and I suppose they must have stayed loyal to him because they were assured of good-quality fruit. He had a way with him – I had to admit that. He called every woman 'madam' for a start, even those who obviously weren't, but when he said it, it didn't sound like flattery, or like he was patronising them. It just sounded polite in an old-fashioned way. He had a great line in chat as well. If he didn't know them it was usually some remark about the weather, but if he did, he would ask about their families or make jokes, always cutting his cloth according to his audience. When a gaggle of local women were in, it was all 'Now, come on, ladies, get your grapes. Sweetest you can taste. Just the thing for putting passion into your marriage,' or 'Best bananas – good enough to eat sideways.' They all loved it, and I'm sure it was good for business. Whatever their bills came to, he always gave them back the few odd pence, and I'm sure they thought he was very generous. As far as I was concerned, I thought he was one of the meanest men I'd ever met. For a start, he never threw anything away – that was one of the things that was wrong with the shop. Whether it was a bit of string or a piece of wood, he stored it carefully, and if he saw me about to throw something away, he'd stop me with a 'Never know when it might come in useful, son.' Most of the produce he collected himself from the market early in the morning, but whenever deliveries were made, he inspected each consignment rigorously, with an energy that frequently exasperated the deliverer. If he found a damaged piece of fruit, he would hold it up for mutual observation and, wrestling up his trousers with the other hand, would say something like, 'Now come on George, are you trying to put me out of business?' and he'd haggle anew over already arranged prices. Watching him sniffing out flawed produce would have made you think he'd an in-built radar system. And he was always looking for something for nothing. Sometimes it was embarrassing. If the Antrim Road had still had horses going up and down it, he'd have been out collecting the droppings and selling them for manure.

One day Father Hennessy came into the shop. Mr Breen's face dropped noticeably and about half a dozen parts of his body seemed to fidget all at once.

'Hello, Father. What can I do for you?'

'Hello, Gerry. How's business?'

'Slow, Father, very slow.'

The priest smiled and, lifting an apple, rubbed it on his sleeve, the red bright against the black.

'I'm popping over to the Mater to visit some parishioners. I thought a nice parcel of fruit would cheer them up. Help them to get better.'

He started to eat the apple and his eyes were smiling.

'Of course, Father. A very good idea.'

With well-disguised misery, he parcelled up a variety of fruit and handed it over the counter.

'God bless you, Gerry. Treasure in heaven, treasure in heaven.'

With the package tucked under his arm, and still eating the apple, the priest sauntered out to his car. If he had looked back, he would have seen Mr Breen slumped on the counter, his head resting on both hands.

'The church'll be the ruin of me. He does that about three times a month. Thinks my name's Mr Del Monte, not Gerry Breen. Treasure in heaven's no use to me when I go to pay the bills at the end of the month.'

The frustration poured out of him and I listened in silence, knowing he wasn't really talking to me.

'Does he go up to Michael Devlin in the bank and ask him for some money because he's going to visit the poor? Since when did it become part of my purpose in life to subsidise the National Health system? I pay my taxes like anyone else.'

I think he'd have gone on indefinitely in a similar vein, but for the arrival of a customer, and then it was all smiles and jokes about the rain.

'Do you know, Mrs Caskey, what I and my assistant are building out in the yard?'

Mrs Caskey didn't know but her aroused curiosity was impatient for an answer.

'We're building an ark! And whenever it's finished we're going to load up two of every type of fruit and float away up the road.'

'Get away with you, Gerry. You're a desperate man.'

And then he sold her tomatoes and a lettuce which he described as 'the best lettuce in the shop.' I'd almost have believed him myself, but for the fact that I'd already heard the same phrase on about three previous occasions that day.

Gerry Breen was very proud of his shop, but he took a special pride in his displays outside, and he did this expert printing with whitening on the front window. Not only did he fancy himself a bit of an artist, but also as a kind of poet laureate among fruiterers. He had all these bits of cardboard – I think they were backing cards out of shirts – and on them he printed, not only the names and prices of the fruit, but also descriptive phrases meant to stimulate the taste-buds of the reader. Grapes might be described as 'deliciously sweet' or strawberries as 'the sweet taste of summer' while Comber spuds were always 'balls of flour.' The front window always looked well. Bedded on a gentle slope of simulated grass rested the various sections of produce, complete with printed labels. Each morning when he had arranged it he would go out on the pavement and stand with his hands on his hips, studying it like an art critic viewing a painting. Inside he had other signs saying things like 'Reach for a peach,' 'Iceberg lettuce – just a tip of the selection' or 'Fancy an apple – why not eat a pear?'

After the first week or so we started to get on a little better. I think he realised that I was trustworthy and prepared to pull my weight. He probably thought of me as being a bit snobbish, but tolerated it so long as he got good value for his money. I in turn became less critical of what I considered his defects. Gradually, he began to employ more of my time on less menial jobs. After three weeks I had progressed to serving customers and weighing their fruit, and then a week later I was allowed to enter the holy of holies and put my hand in the till. I still had to chop sticks and brush up, of course, but whenever the shop was busy I served behind the counter. I almost began to feel part of the business. The continual wet weather stopped me from missing out on the usual activities of summer and I was increasingly optimistic that my father would reward my industry with a motorbike. Mr Breen didn't much like the rain – he was always complaining how bad it was for business. According to him, it discouraged passing trade, and people didn't buy as much as they did in warm weather. He was probably right. Sometimes, when a lull in trade created boredom, I tried to wind him up a little.

'Mr Breen, do you not think it's wrong to sell South African fruit?'

'Aw, don't be daft, son.'

'But do you not think that by selling their fruit you're supporting apartheid?'

He swapped his pencil from ear to ear and did what looked a bit like a tap-dance.

'I'm only supporting myself and the wife. Sure, wouldn't the blacks be the first to suffer if I stopped selling it? They'd all end up starving, and how would that help them?'

I was about to provoke him further when a customer appeared and I let him have the last word.

'God knows, son, they have my sympathy – don't I work like a black myself?'

The customer turned out to be Mr Breen's wife. She was all dressed up in a blue and white suit and was on her way to some social function. She had one of those golden charm bracelets that clunked so many heavy charms I wondered how her wrist bore the strain, and while she hardly looked sideways at him, she made an embarrassing fuss over me, asking about my parents and school, and gushing on in a slightly artificial way. When she finished whatever business she had, she said goodbye to me and warned Gerald not to work me too hard. I smiled at the name Gerald, and I could see him squirming behind the counter. A heavy shower came on and we both stood in the doorway watching it bounce off the road. He was unusually silent and I glanced at him a few times to see if he was all right. When he spoke, his voice was strangely colourless.

'Never get married, son – it's the end of your happiness.'

I didn't know whether he was joking or not, so I just went on staring at the rain.

'My wife's ashamed of me,' he said in the same lifeless voice.

I uttered some vague and unconvincing disagreement and then turned away in embarrassment. I started to brush the floor, glancing up from time to time as he stood motionless in the doorway. In a minute or so the rain eased and it seemed to break the spell, but for the rest of that afternoon, he was subdued and functioned in a mechanical way. He even closed the shop half an hour early – something he'd never done before.

Nothing like that ever happened again, my first experience of work slipped into an uneventful routine. One day, though, comes clearly to mind. One afternoon when business was slack he asked me to deliver fruit round to a Mrs McCausland. The address was a couple of streets away and I felt a little self-conscious as I set off in my green coat. It wasn't a big order – just a few apples and oranges and things. I followed the directions I had been given and arrived at a terraced house. Unlike most of its neighbours, the front door was closed, and the net curtain in the window offered no glimpse of the interior. At first, it seemed as if no one was in, and I was just about to turn and leave, when there was the slow undrawing of a bolt and the rattle of a chain. The door opened wide enough to allow an old woman's face to peer out at me, suspicion speckling her eyes. I identified myself and showed the fruit to reassure her. Then there was another pause before the door gradually opened to reveal an old woman leaning heavily on a walking stick. Inviting me in, she hobbled off slowly and painfully down the hall and into her tiny living-room. She made me sit down and, despite my polite protests, proceeded to make me a cup of tea. The room resembled a kind of grotto, adorned with religious objects and pictures. Her rosary beads hung from the fireplace clock and a black cat slept on the rug-covered sofa. She talked to me from the kitchen as she worked.

'Isn't the weather terrible?'

'Desperate – you'd never think it was the summer,' I replied, smiling as I listened to myself. I had started to sound like Gerry Breen's apprentice.

'Summers never used to be like this. I can remember summers when the streets were baked hot as an oven and everyone used to sit on their doorsteps for you could hardly get a breath. If you sat on your doorstep these past few days you'd get pneumonia.'

She brought me a cup of tea in a china cup, and a slice of fruit cake, but nothing for herself. She sat down and scrutinised me intently.

'So you're working for Gerry for the summer. I'm sure that's good fun for you. You work hard and maybe he'll keep you on permanent.'

I didn't correct her misunderstanding, but I laughed silently inside.

'He says if it keeps on raining he's going to start building an ark.'

She smiled and rearranged the cushion supporting her back.

'Gerry's the salt of the earth. Do you see that fruit you brought? He's been doing that for the best part of fifteen years and nobody knows but him and me.'

She paused to pour more tea into my cup and I listened with curiosity as she continued, her words making me feel as if I was looking at a familiar object from a new and unexpected perspective.

'I gave him a wee bit of help a long time ago and he's never forgotten it, not through all these years. I don't get out much now, but sometimes I take a walk round to the shop, just to see how he's getting on. He's a great man for the crack, isn't he?'

I smiled in agreement and she shuffled forward in her seat, leaning confidentially towards me.

'Have you met Lady Muck yet? Thon woman's more airs and graces than royalty. She was born and bred a stone's throw from here and to listen to her now you'd think she came from the Malone Road. I knew her family and they didn't have two pennies to rub together between the lot of them. Now she traipses round the town like she was a duchess. You'll never catch her serving behind the counter.'

It was obvious that the woman wanted to talk – she was probably starved of company – and no matter how often I attempted a polite exit, she insisted on my staying a little longer, assuring me that Gerry wouldn't mind. I wasn't so sure, but there was no easy escape, as she produced a photograph album and talked me through a maze of memories and mementoes.

Parts of it were interesting and when she told me about the Belfast blitz I learned things I hadn't known before. Before I finally got up to go, she returned to the subject of the weather, her voice serious and solemn.

'This weather's a sign. I've been reading about it in a tract that was sent to me. It's by this holy scholar, very high up in the Church, and he says we're living in the last days. All these wars and famines – they're all signs. All this rain – it's a sign too. I believe it.'

When she opened the front door it was still raining and I almost started to believe it too. I ran back quickly, partly to get out of the rain and partly because I anticipated a rebuke about the length of my absence.

There were no customers in the shop when I entered and he merely lifted his head from what he was reading, asked if everything was all right with Mrs McCausland, and returned to his study. It surprised me a little that he said nothing about the time. He was filling in his pools coupon and concentrating on winning a fortune, so perhaps he was distracted by the complexities of the Australian leagues. He had been doing them all summer and his approach never varied. He did two columns every week, the first by studying the form and this forced him to ponder such probabilities as whether Inala City would draw with Slacks Creek, or Altona with Bulleen. For the second column, he selected random numbers, his eyes screwed up and an expression on his face as if he was waiting for some kind of celestial message. On this particular afternoon, reception must have been bad, because he asked me to shout them out. Out of genuine curiosity, I asked him what he would do if he did win a fortune. He looked at me to see if I was winding him up, but must have sensed that I wasn't, because, on a wet and miserable Belfast afternoon, he told me his dream.

'It's all worked out in here,' he said, tapping the side of his head with a chisel-shaped finger. 'I've it all planned out. Thinking about it keeps you going – makes you feel better on days like this.'

He paused to check if I was laughing at him, then took a hand out of his coat pocket and gestured slowly round the shop.

'Look around you, son. What do you see?'

A still, grey light seemed to have filtered into the shop. The lights were off and it was quiet in an almost eerie way. Nothing rustled or stirred, and the only sound was the soft fall of the rain. In the gloom the bright colours smouldered like embers; rhubarb like long tongues of flame; red sparks of apples; peaches, perfect in their velvety softness, yellows and oranges flickering gently.

'Fruit,' I answered. 'Different kinds of fruit.'

'Now, do you know what I see?'

I shook my head.

'I see places. A hundred different places. Look again.' And as he spoke he began to point with his finger. 'Oranges from Spain, apples from New Zealand, cabbages from Holland, peaches from Italy, grapes from the Cape, bananas from Ecuador – fruit from all over the world. Crops grown and harvested by hands I never see, packed and transported by other hands in a chain that brings them here to me. It's a miracle if you think about it. When we're sleeping in our beds, hands all over the world are packing and picking so that Gerry Breen can sell it here in this shop.'

We both stood and looked, absorbing the magnitude of the miracle.

'You asked me what I'd do if I won the jackpot – well, I've got it all thought out. I'd go to every country whose fruit I sell, go and see it grow, right there in the fields and the groves, in the orchards and the vineyards. All over the world!'

He looked at me out of the corner of his eye to see if I thought he was crazy, then turned away and began to tidy the counter. I didn't say anything, but in that moment, if he'd asked me, I would have gone with him. All these years later, I still regret that I didn't tell him that. Told him while there was still time.

Four days later, Gerry Breen was dead. A man walked into the shop and shot him twice. He became another bystander, another nobody, sucked into the vortex by a random and malignant fate that marked him out. They needed a Catholic to balance the score – he became a casualty of convenience, a victim of retribution, propitiation of a different god. No one even claimed it. Just one more sectarian murder – unclaimed, unsolved, soon unremembered but by a few. A name lost in the anonymity of a long list. I would forget too, but I can't.

I remember it all. There were no customers when a motorbike stopped outside with two men on it. The engine was still running as the passenger came towards the shop. I was behind the counter looking out. He had one hand inside his black motorcycle tunic and wore a blue crash-helmet – the type that encloses the whole head. A green scarf covered the bottom half of his face, so only his eyes were visible. Only his eyes – that's all I ever saw of him. Mr Breen was standing holding a tray of oranges he had just brought from the back.

Suddenly, the man pulled a gun out of his tunic and I thought we were going to be robbed, but he never spoke, and as he raised the gun and pointed at Mr Breen, his hand was shaking so much he had to support it with the other one. It was then I knew he hadn't come for money. The first shot hit Gerry Breen in the chest, spinning him round, and as he slumped to the floor the oranges scattered and rolled in all directions. He lay there, face down, and his body was still moving. Then, as I screamed an appeal for mercy, the man walked forward and, kneeling over the body, shot him in the back of the head. His body kicked and shuddered, and then was suddenly and unnaturally still. I screamed again in fear and anger and then, pointing the gun at me, the man walked slowly backwards to the door of the shop, ran to the waiting bike and was gone. Shaking uncontrollably and stomach heaving with vomit, I tried to turn Mr Breen over on to his back, but he was too heavy for me. Blood splashed his green coat, and flowed from the dark gaping wound, streaming across the floor, mixing with the oranges that were strewn all around us. Oranges from Spain.

They say help arrived almost immediately. I don't know. All I can remember is thinking of the old woman's words and hoping it really was the end of the world, and being glad and asking God to drown the world, wanting it to rain for a thousand years, rain and rain and never stop until all the blood was washed away and every street was washed clean. There were voices then and helping hands trying to lift me away, but no one could move me as I knelt beside him, clutching frantically at his green coat, begging God not to let him die, praying he'd let Gerry Breen live to build his ark and bring aboard the fruit of the world. All the fruit of the world safely stored. Oranges from Spain, apples from the Cape – the sweet taste of summer preserved for ever, eternal and incorruptible.

Belfast Woman

MARY BECKETT 1980

In the city of Belfast almost all Catholics and Protestants lived, and continue to live, in separate communities. In times of high tension these communities can be the objects of attack by extremists from the other side. Some families experience this several times in their lives; some leave, to resettle in areas where people of their own religion live. But in this tale a woman refuses to give in and, in her grim courage, signals that it may be possible not to yield to violence – provided one has the gift of dour realism and strong independence.

I mind well the day the threatening letter came. It was a bright morning, and warm, and I remember thinking while I was dressing myself that it would be nice if the Troubles were over so that a body could just enjoy the feel of a good day. When I came down the stairs the hall was dark but I could see the letter lying face down. I lifted it and just my name was on the envelope, 'Mrs Harrison' in red felt pen. I knew what it was. There was a page of an exercise book inside with 'Get out or we'll burn you out' all in red with bad printing and smeared. I just went in and sat at the kitchen table with the note in front of me. I never made myself a cup of tea even. It was a shock, though God knows I shouldn't have been surprised.

One of the first things I remember in my life was wakening up with my mother screaming downstairs when we were burnt out in 1921. I ran down in my nightgown and my mother was standing in the middle of the kitchen with her hands up to her face screaming and screaming and the curtains were on fire and my father was pulling them down and stamping on them with the flames catching the oilcloth on the floor. Then he shouted: 'Sadie, the children,' and she stopped screaming and said: 'Oh God, Michael, the children,' and she ran upstairs and came down with the baby in one arm and Joey under the other, and my father took Joey in his arms and me by the hand and we ran out along the street. It was a warm summer night and the fires were crackling all over the place and the street was covered with broken glass. It wasn't until we got into my grandmother's house that anybody noticed that I had nothing on but my nightie and nothing on my feet and they were cut. It was all burnt, everything they had. My mother used to say she didn't save as much as a needle and thread. I wasn't able to sleep for weeks, afraid I'd be wakened by that screaming.

We stayed in my grandmother's house until 1935 and my grandmother was dead by that time and my father too for he got TB like many another then. He used to say 'When you have no house and no job, sure what use are you?' and then he'd get fits of coughing. In 1935 when we got the letter threatening to burn us out I said to my mother: 'We'll gather our things and we'll go.' So we did and like all the rest of them in our street we went up to Glenard to the new houses. When we showed our 'Get out or we'll burn you out' note they gave us a house and we'd enough out to get things fixed up. We got new jobs in another mill, my mother and Patsy and me. Only my mother never liked it there. She always said the air was too strong for her. It was cold right enough, up close to the mountains. But when I was getting married to William, and his aunt who was a Protestant gave him the key of her house in this street, my mother was in a terrible state – 'Don't go into that Protestant street, Mary, or you'll be a sorry girl,' and she said we could live with her. But I didn't want William to pine like my poor father, so here we came and not a day's trouble until the note came.

Mind you, the second night we were here there was trouble in the Catholic streets across the road. We heard shots first and then the kind of rumbling, roaring noises of all the people out on the streets. I wanted to get up and run out and see what was wrong but William held on to me in bed and he said: 'They don't run out on the street here. They stay in.' And it was true. They did. I was scared lying listening to the noise the way I never was when I was out with my neighbours. It turned out some poor young lad had stayed at home when he should have gone back to the British army and they sent the police for him. He got out of the back window and ran down the entry and the police ran after him and shot him dead. They said their gun went off by accident but the people said they beat him up. When I went over the next day I saw him laid out in the wee room off the kitchen and his face had all big yellowy-greenish blotches on it. I never mentioned it to my new neighbours, and they never mentioned it to me.

I couldn't complain about them. They were good decent people. They didn't come into the house for a chat or a loan of tea or milk or sugar like the neighbours in Glenard or North Queen Street but they were ready to help at any time. I didn't know the men much because they had work so they didn't stand around the corners the way I was used to. But when Liam was born they all helped and said what a fine baby he was. He was too. Nine pounds with black hair and so strong he could lift his head and look round at a week old. They were always remarking on his mottled skin – purply kind of measles when he'd be up out of the pram – and said it was the sign of a very strong baby. At that time I had never seen a baby with any other colour of skin – I suppose Catholic babies had to be strong to get by. But when Eileen was born a year and ten months later she was different. She had beautiful creamy skin. She was plump and perfect and I loved her more than Liam, God forgive me, and more than William and more than anybody in the world and I wanted everything to be right for her. I thought to myself if I was a Protestant now we'd have just the two and no more and I'd be able to look after them and do well for them. So I didn't act fair with William at all.

Then I started having trouble. I looked as if I was expecting again and my stomach was hard and round but I had bleeding and I could feel no life so I was afraid. I went to the doctor and he said, 'No, Mrs Harrison, you're not pregnant. There is something here we shall have to look into.' And I said, 'Is it serious, doctor?' and he said, 'I can't tell you that, can I, until you go into hospital and have it investigated' and I said, 'Do you mean an operation?' and he said, 'I do, Mrs Harrison.' I came home saying to myself it's cancer and who will rear my Eileen and Liam. I remembered hearing it said that once they put the knife into you, you were dead in six months so I made up my mind I'd have no operation and I'd last out as long as I could. Every year I was able to look after them would be a year gained and the bigger they were the better they'd be able to do without me. But, oh dear, it was terrible hard on everybody. I told William and my mother and Patsy there was nothing at all the matter with me but they knew to look at me it wasn't true. I was a real blay colour and I was so tired I was ready to drop. I'd sit down by the fire at night when the children were in bed and my eyes would close and if I opened them I'd see William staring at me with such a tortured look on his face I'd have to close them again so that I wouldn't go and lean my head against him and tell him the whole thing. I knew if I did that he'd make me go back to the doctor and I'd be done for. At times I'd see against my closed eyes the white long roots of the cancer growing all over my inside and I'd remember the first time William brought me to see his father in the country.

He had a fine labourer's cottage for he was a Protestant and was head ploughman to some rich farmer down there. He was a good man. William's mother was a Catholic and she died when William was a wee boy but they brought him up a Catholic because it had been promised. He was cross-looking, though, and I was a bit nervous of him. He had his garden all planted in rows and squares and he was digging clods in one corner and breaking them up fine and I could see all the long white roots and threads he was shaking the mud out of and he turned to us and he said: 'Sitfast and scutch! Sitfast and scutch! They're the plague of my life. No matter how much I weed there's more in the morning.' I told him about my grandfather and the big elderberry tree that grew behind the wee house he'd got in the country when he was burnt out in Lisburn. It wasn't there when he went into the house and when he noticed it first it was only a wee bit of a bush but it grew so quickly it blocked out all the light from his back window. Then one summer it was covered with black slimy kind of flies so he cut it down to the stump, but it started growing again straight away. One day when my father took Patsy and Joey and me down to visit him he had dug all around the stump and he was trying to pull it out with a rope. He told my father to pull with him. My father tried but then he leaned against the wall with his face pale and covered with sweat. My grandfather said: 'Are you finished, Michael?' and my father said, 'I'm clean done,' and my grandfather said, 'God help us all' and brought us into the house and gave us lemonade. It was just after that my father went into the sanatorium and my mother was all the time bringing him bottles of lemonade. At the funeral I asked my grandfather if he got the stump out and he didn't know for a minute what I was talking about. Then he said, 'No, no. Indeed the rope's still lying out there. I must bring it in or it'll rot.' I never saw him again, never saw the wee house either. My mother never was one for the country.

She wasn't old herself when she died – not that much over fifty, but she looked an old woman. She wore a shawl at times and not many did that any more. She was always fussing about my health and me going to the doctor but I managed fine without. I didn't look much. I had this swollen stomach and I got into the way of hiding it with my arms. But every year I got through I'd say to myself wasn't I right to stick it out. When the war finished and the free health came, everybody thought I'd get myself seen to, and my mother was at me she'd mind Liam and Eileen. Of course there were no more children but I kept those two lovely. There was no Protestant child better fed or better dressed than those two, and I always warned them to fight with nobody, never to get into trouble. If any of the children started to shout at them about being Catholics or Fenians or Teagues they were just to walk away, not to run mind you, but just walk home. And Liam was the best boy ever. He wasn't great at his lessons but the masters said how pleasant and good he was. Eileen was inclined to be a bit bold and that was the cause of the only terrible thing I ever did. I can't believe even now how I came to do it. It was the week after my mother had died.

I blamed myself for what happened to my mother. I should have seen in time that she wasn't well and made her mind herself and she'd have lasted better. She came into my house one day with her shawl on and I was going to say I wished she'd wear a coat and not have my neighbours passing remarks, but she hung the shawl up on the back of the door and she looked poorly. She said she'd had a terrible pain in her chest and she had been to the doctor and he'd told her it was her heart. She was to rest and take tablets. She had other wee tablets to put under her tongue if she got a pain and she was not to go up hills. She looked so bad I put her to bed in the wee room off the kitchen. She never got up again. She had tense crushing pains and the tablets did no good. Sometimes the sip of Lourdes water helped her. The doctor said he could do nothing for her unless she went into hospital and she wouldn't hear of that. 'Ah no, no. I'm just done, that's all.' Every now and again she'd say this would never have happened if she hadn't been burnt out of her home down near the docks and had to go half roads up the mountains with all the hills and the air too strong for her. 'And your father wouldn't ever have got consumption if he hadn't had to move in with my mother and spend his days at the street corner. You wouldn't remember it, Mary. You were too small,' she'd say and I never contradicted her, 'but we hadn't left as much as a needle and thread. The whole block went up. Nothing left.' She was buried from our house even though she kept saying she must go home. She had a horror of my Protestant neighbours even though she liked well enough the ones she met. But at her funeral, better kinder decenter neighbours you could not get. When it was over, all I could do was shiver inside myself as if my shelter had been taken away. William was good to me, always good to me, but I had to keep a bit of myself to myself with him. My mother never looked for anything from me. I'd tell her what I needed to tell her and she'd listen, but she never interfered. And she was as proud of Liam and Eileen as I was. I'd see the way she looked at them.

The week after she died Eileen came home from school crying. She was ten years of age and she didn't often cry. She showed me the mark on her legs where the headteacher had hit her with a cane. A big red mark it was right across the back of her legs. And she had lovely skin on her legs, lovely creamy skin. When I think of it I can still see that mark. I didn't ask her what happened. I just lifted my mother's shawl from where it was still hanging on the back of the kitchen door and I flung it round me and ran down to the school. I knocked the door and she opened it herself, the head-teacher, because the most of the school had gone home. She took one look at me and ran away back into a classroom. I went after her. She ran into another room off it and banged the door. My arm stuck in through the glass panel and I pulled it out with a big deep cut from my wrist to my elbow. She didn't come out of the door and I never spoke to her at all. There were a couple of other teachers over a bit and a few children about but I couldn't say anything to anybody and they just stood. To stop the blood pouring so much I held my arm up out of my mother's shawl as I went back up the street. There was a woman standing at her door near the top of the street. She was generally at her door knitting, that woman. She had very clever children and some of them did well. One got to be a teacher, another was in the Post Office which is about as far as a clever poor Catholic can get. She asked me what happened but when I couldn't answer she said, 'You'd need to get to the hospital, Mrs. I'll get my coat and go with you.' I didn't want to go to any hospital. I just wanted to go home and wash off all the blood but my head was spinning so I let myself be helped on the bus. They stitched it up and wanted me to stay in for the night but I was terrified they'd operate on me just when I was managing so well. I insisted I couldn't because the children were on their own and Mrs O'Reilly came with me right to the end of my own street. 'If your neighbours ask what happened, just tell them you fell off the bus,' she told me. 'You don't want them knowing all about your business.' I've heard she was from the west of Ireland.

When I went into the kitchen I was ready to drop but Eileen started screaming and crying and saying how ashamed of me she was and that she'd never go back to school again. Liam made me a cup of tea and stood looking worried at me. When William came in from work he helped me to bed and was kind and good but I could see by the cut of his mouth that he was shocked and offended at me. It took a long time to heal and the scar will never leave me. The story went around the parish in different ways. Some said I hit the teacher. Some said she knifed me. I was too ashamed ever to explain.

Eileen never was touched in school after that, though, and when she left she learned shorthand and typing and got an office job. She grew up lovely, and I used to think, watching her going out in the morning in the best of clothes with her hair shining, that she could have gone anywhere and done herself credit. She wasn't contented living where we did. At first I didn't understand what she wanted. I thought she wanted a better house in a better district. I didn't know how we could manage it but I made up my mind it would have to be done. I went for walks up round the avenues where there were detached houses with gardens and when I saw an empty house I'd peer in through the windows. Then one day a woman from the parish, who worked cleaning one of those houses, saw me and asked me in because the people of the house were out all day. Seeing it furnished with good solid shining furniture I knew we'd never manage it. In the sitting-room there was an old-fashioned copper canopy and when I looked into it I could see the whole room reflected smaller like a fairy-tale with flowers and books and pictures and plates on the wall. I knew it wasn't for us. How could I go in and out there? William and Liam wouldn't look right in their working clothes. Only Eileen would fit in. I was a bit sad but relieved because at no time could I see where the money would have come from. I told her that night when she came in but she looked at me all puzzled. 'But that wasn't what I meant, Mammy,' she said. 'I have to get away from everything here. There's no life for me here. I'm thinking of going to Canada.' That was before any trouble at all here. People now would say that was in the good times when you could get in a bus and go round the shops or into the pictures and nothing would have happened by the time you came home except that the slack would have burnt down a bit on the fire.

Off she went anyway and got a job and wrote now and again telling us how well-off she was. In no time at all she was married and was sending photographs first of this lovely bungalow and then of her two wee girls with the paddling pool in her garden or at their swing when they were a bit bigger. I was glad she was doing so well. It was the kind of life I had reared her for and dreamed of for her, only I wished she and her children were not so far away. I kept inviting her home for a visit but I knew it would cost far too much money. Only I thought if she was homesick it would help her to know we wanted to see her too. Once the troubles came I stopped asking her.

Liam at that time was getting on well too. He was always such a nice pleasant big fellow that a plumber in the next street to ours asked him to join in his business at putting in fireplaces and hot-water pipes. He put in a lovely fireplace for me with a copper canopy like the one I'd seen years before and built me a bathroom and hot water and put in a sink unit for me till I was far better off than any of my neighbours even though a lot of them had their houses very nice too. They were able to get paint from the shipyard, of course, and marble slabs and nice bits of mahogany. He got married to a nice wee girl from the Bone and they got a house up in one of the nice streets in Ardoyne – up the far end in what they call now a mixed area. It's all gone now, poor Liam's good way of living. When that street of houses up there was put on fire in 1972 his wife Gemma insisted on coming back to the Bone and squatting in an empty house. They did their best to fix it up but it's old and dark. Then when the murders got bad his partner asked him not to come back to work any more because he'd been threatened for working with a Catholic. I was raging when Liam told me, raging about what a coward the plumber was but then, as Liam said, you can't blame a man for not wanting to be murdered. So there he is – no work and no house and a timid wife and a family of lovely wee children. He had plenty to put up with. But where else could I go when I got the note? I sat looking round my shining kitchen and the note said 'Get out or we'll burn you out' and where could I go for help but to Liam?

Still I was glad William was dead before it happened. He would have been so annoyed. He felt so ashamed when the Protestants did something nasty. I could swallow my own shame every time the IRA disgraced us. I lived with it the same as I lived with the memory of my own disgrace when I went for the teacher and ripped my arm. But William had always been such a good upright man, he could never understand wickedness. Even the way he died showed it. He was a carter all his days, always in steady work but for a while before he died they were saying to him that nobody had horses any more and they were changing to a lorry. He could never drive a lorry. He was afraid he'd be on the dole. It wasn't the money he was worrying about for I kept telling him it would make little difference to us – just the two of us, what did it matter? It was his pride that was upset. For years there was a big notice up on a corner shop at the bottom of the Oldpark Road. It said: 'Drivers, dismount. Don't overload your horses going up the hill.' He used to remark on it. It irked him if he didn't obey it. So one day in March when there was an east wind he collapsed on the hill and died the next day in hospital with the same disease as my mother.

There was a young doctor in the hospital asked me did I need a tranquilliser or a sleeping tablet or something to get over the shock. I told him no, that I never took any tablets, that I had had cancer when I was in my twenties and that I was still alive in my fifties with never a day in bed. He was curious and he asked me questions and then he said, 'Mrs Harrison, of course I can't be absolutely sure, but I'd say it was most unlikely you had cancer. Maybe you needed a job done on your womb. Maybe you even needed your womb removed but I would be very, very surprised if you had cancer. You wouldn't be here now if you had.' So I went in and knelt down at William's side. He still had that strained, worried look, even then. All I could think was: 'Poor William. Poor William. Poor, poor, poor William.'

It wasn't that I was lonely without him for I'd kept him at a distance for a long time, but the days had no shape to them. I could have my breakfast, dinner and tea whatever time I liked or I needn't have them at all. For a while I didn't bother cooking for myself, just ate tea and bread. Then Liam's wife, Gemma, said the butcher told her that I hadn't darkened his door since William died and that if I wouldn't cook for myself I'd have to come and have my dinner with them. So I thought to myself I wasn't being sensible and I'd only be a nuisance to them if I got sick so I fixed everything to the clock as if there was no such thing as eternity. Until that morning the note came and then I just sat, I didn't look at the clock. I didn't make a cup of tea. I didn't know how long I stayed. I felt heavy, not able to move. Then I thought maybe Liam could get somebody with a van to take out my furniture and I could think later where to go. I took my rosary beads from under my pillow and my handbag with my money and my pension book and Eileen's letters and the photographs of her children and I shut the door behind me. There wasn't a soul in the street but there was nothing odd about that. You'll always know you're in a Protestant street if it's deserted. When I went across the road to get to Liam's house there were children playing and men at the corner and women standing at the doors in the sun and a squad of nervous-looking soldiers down at the other end.

Liam wasn't in but Gemma and the children were. The breakfast table wasn't cleared and Gemma was feeding the youngest. When he finished she stood him up on her lap and he reached over her shoulder trying to reach the shiny new handle Liam had put on the door. He was sturdy and happy and he had a warm smell of milk and baby-powder. I wanted to hold him but I was afraid of putting her out of her routine. Sometimes I wonder if she has a routine – compared to the way I reared mine. Nothing was allowed to interrupt their feeding times and sleeping times. Maybe I was wrong and I'll never know what way Eileen managed hers. I would have liked to do the dishes too but I was afraid it might look like criticising. After a wee while chatting Gemma got up to put the child in his pram and make us a cup of tea. 'You don't look great, Granny,' she said. 'Are you minding yourself at all?' I opened my bag and showed her the note.

She screamed and put her hands up to her face and the baby was startled and cried and bounced up and down in his pram with his arms up to be lifted. I said, 'Don't scream, Gemma. Don't ever scream, do you hear me,' and I unstrapped the baby and hugged him. She stared at me, surprised, and it stopped her. 'You'll have to come and stay here,' she said. 'We'll fit you in.' She gave a kind of a look around and I could see her thinking where on earth she could fit me in. Still, where could I go? 'All I wanted was for Liam to get a van and take out my stuff,' I explained. 'Maybe my sister Patsy would have more room than you.' She took the baby and gave me my cup of tea. 'You'll come here,' she said. 'You'll count this your home and we'll be glad to have you.' She was a good kind girl, Gemma, and when Liam came in he was the same; only anxious to make me welcome and he went off to get the van.

After a while Gemma said, 'Write to Eileen straight away. She's the one you should be living with anyway – not all alone over yonder. All her money and her grand house. She's the one should have you.' I laughed but it hurt me a bit to hear it said. 'What would I do in Eileen's grand house in Canada? How would I fit in?' And Gemma said: 'You could keep her house all shining. She'd use you for that. Where would you see the like of your own house for polish! You'd do great for Eileen.' I looked round her own few bits and pieces – no look on anything, and a pile of children's clothes on the floor waiting to be washed and the children running in and out and knocking things over. Mary, my wee Godchild, came and stood leaning against my knees, sucking her thumb. She was wearing one of the dresses I make for them. In the spring when I was fitting it on her I was noticing how beautiful her skin was with little pinprick freckles on the pink and white and I was thinking when she's so lovely what must Eileen's children be like. Then she turned her head and looked at me and her eyes were full of love – for me! I couldn't get over it. Since then sometimes she'd just hold my hand. When Liam came back I said, 'Liam, I'm going home. I'm sorry about the bother. I just got frightened but you can cancel the van. I'm going home and I'm staying home. I've a Protestant house to the right of me and Protestant house to the left of me. They'll not burn me out.' They argued with me and they were a bit upset but I knew they were relieved and I stuck to it.

Liam insisted on going back to the house with me although since the murders started I had never let him come down my side of the road. There was a land-rover with soldiers in it not far from my door and no flames, no smoke. But when I opened the door, such a mess. There was water spouting out of a broken pipe in the wall where they had pulled out my sink. The Sacred Heart statue and the wee red lamp were broken on the floor. My copper canopy was all dinged. The table had big hatchet marks on it. The cover on the couch was ripped and the stuffing pulled out. And filth. For months I thought I could get the smell of that filth. I wouldn't let Liam turn off the water until I had it washed away. We cleaned up a bit but Liam said he'd have to get help before he could do much and not to touch the electric because the water had got into it. He had been very quiet so I jumped when he shouted at the soldiers once he went out the door. They drove up very slowly and he was shouting and waving his arms and calling them names. One of them looked into the house and started to laugh. Liam yelled at him about me being a widow woman living alone and that they were here to protect me but one of them said, 'You've got it wrong. We're here to wipe out the IRA.'

'Oh, Liam,' I said 'go home. Go home before harm befalls you,' and he shook his fist at the soldiers and shouted, 'I'm going now but I'll be back and I won't be on my own then. Just look out. I'm warning you.' He turned and ran off down the street and the soldier turned and looked after him and I thought he was lifting up his gun and I grabbed at his arm and the gun went off into the air and I begged, 'Don't shoot at him. Oh don't shoot him.' He said, 'Mrs, I have no intention . . .' and then I fell against the wall and when I came to they were making me drink whiskey out of a bottle. It made me cough and splutter but it brought me round. They weren't bad to me, I must admit. When I was on my feet they corked up the bottle and put it back in the land-rover and drove off. Not one of my neighbours came out and all evening when I worked at tidying up and all night when I sat up to keep watch, not one of them knocked at my door.

Next day Liam brought back two other lads and they fixed up the electricity and the water. It took a while to get everything decent again but they were in and out every day, sometimes three or four of them and it never cost me a penny. Then a queer thing happened. My neighbours began moving out. The woman next door told me out of the side of her mouth that they had all been threatened. I didn't understand how a whole Protestant area could be threatened but out they all went. Of course I know they can always get newer better houses when they ask for them and indeed there was a lot of shooting and wrecking on the front of the road, but still I often wondered what was the truth of it. Maybe I'm better off not knowing. As they left, Catholics from across the road moved in – mostly older people and I have good friends among them, although it took us a while to get used to each other. I didn't take easy to people expecting to open my door and walk in at any hour of the day. They thought I was a bit stiff. I have no time for long chats and I never liked gossip. But Mrs Mulvenna, next door now, has a son in Australia – farther away than my Eileen and I think sons are even worse at writing home. I listen to her and I feel for her and I show her my photographs. I didn't tell her when Eileen wrote about how ashamed she was of us all and how she didn't like to let on she was Irish. I see talk like that in the papers too. It's not right to put the blame on poor powerless people. The most of us never did anything but stay quiet and put up with things the way they were. And we never taught our children to hate the others nor filled their heads with their wrongs the way it's said we did. When all the young people thought they could fix everything with marches and meetings I said it wouldn't work and they laughed at me. 'All you old ones are awful bitter,' they said and they jeered when Hannah in the shop and I were warning them 'It'll all lead to shooting and burning and murder.'

Still, last November a man came round here trying to sell Venetian blinds. Some of the houses have them but I said no I liked to see out. I pointed to the sunset behind Divis – bits of red and yellow in the sky and a sort of mist all down the mountain that made it nearly see-through. The man looked at it for a minute and then he said, 'Do you know Belfast has the most beautiful sunsets in the whole world?' I said I didn't because I'd never been any place close to look at sunsets and he said, 'They tell me Belfast has the best and do you know why? It's because of all the smoke and dirt and dust and pollution. And it seems to me,' he said, 'it seems to me that if the dirt and dust and smoke and pollution of Belfast just with the help of the sun can make a sky like that, then there's hope for all of us.' He nodded and winked and touched his hat and went off and I went in and sat down at the table. And thinking of it I started to laugh, for it's true. There is hope for all of us. Well, anyway, if you don't die you live through it, day in, day out.

Glossary

abandoned	reckless
Adam's last glimpse of Paradise	Biblical: when Adam was driven from Paradise because of his sin
Angry Brigade	a British terrorist group active in the 1960s and 1970s
bagged up	form of 'buggered up'; slightly less offensive
beach-crop	the different seaweeds gathered for food or fertiliser
begor	exclamation; corruption of 'by God'
biretta	a black, brimless hat worn by Catholic priests
bob	slang for a shilling, now replaced by five-pence piece
bog	marshy earth with large area unsafe to walk on
bonnes-bouches	a tasty morsel (French); something savoured with pleasure
boreen	narrow country road
byre	cowshed
caffler	sneak
Carmelite	an order of teaching nuns
carrageen	edible seaweed
changeling	a fairy or goblin child left in exchange for a human child
chosen people	Biblical reference to the Israelites
cock-of-the-walk	the master; in charge
cod	hoax; joke
colleges	private, residential schools
column	guerrilla soldiers, constantly moving to evade the enemy
Confirmation	a ceremony in which adolescents publicly confirm their belief in the teachings of Christianity and are blessed by a bishop
crack	lively, entertaining talk

creel	flat basket with a lid for fish or farmwork
crossed over	crossed the Atlantic to America
crossing oneself	a Christian sign of reverence; the sign of the Cross
delft	glazed earthenware for household use: cups, dishes etc.
Delilah/Samson	Biblical lovers; Delilah seduced Samson and then betrayed him by cutting his hair wherein lay his strength
Del Monte	large fruit importer – exporter
de rigueur	the rule; the accepted custom
detail a section	give orders to a group of soldiers
dispensary	pharmacy
drawing	filling the baskets with seaweed
dulse	edible seaweed typical of the western shores
the Essex	Essex Regiment of British soldiers
ewe lamb	lamb born to a mature sheep; most cherished child
ewer	water jug
family rosary	nightly family prayers using the rosary, a circle of beads to keep count of the prayers said
fanny	bottom
Fatima	a place of pilgrimage in Portugal where the Virgin Mary is said to have appeared
Fenian	derogatory term for Catholic
a flaking	a beating
fluke	flat fish
Friday	in the Catholic Church Friday used to be a day of abstaining from eating meat; to break this rule was a sin
fuchsia	hedges of red-purple flowers, typical of the west of Ireland
garth	paddock or field
gauntlet gloves	gloves with long, wide cuffs above the wrists
Gladstone	19th-century Prime Minister of England who supported Home Rule for Ireland
going out foreign	going abroad

golden calf	the Bible tells how a golden calf was worshipped by people who had turned their backs on God; a false god; the worship of material things
gub	mouth
guinea	an old coin worth just over £1
Hail Mary	a short prayer to ask the protection of the Mother of God
half-crown	a silver coin in old coinage; worth an eighth of a pound
heart-scalded	very upset
hendirt	a tradition of putting some earth, or something connected with the farm, into the trunk of the traveller; this is supposed to hasten the return
hiring fair	a rural labour market where people went to seek employment
hocking	slang for putting in pawn
holy water	water blessed at Easter for baptism and often kept in the home
Home Rule	demand by Irish Members of Parliament for self-government
Indian meal	flour from maize or sweetcorn
IRA	Irish Republican Army
Jay	exclamation; short for 'Jesus'; not disrespectful
July	see Twelfth of July
keen	high-pitched cry of women mourning the dead
knee-capped	IRA punishment; the victim's knee-caps are broken by bullets or other means
Knight of Saint Columbanus	organisation of Catholic businessmen
lead in the joyful mysteries	lead the prayers of the rosary, meditating on joyful events in the Gospels
Leatherwing	name for the heron
Leaving Cert.	final school examination
left-footers	derogatory term for Catholics
Lent	the 40 days before Easter; traditionally a time of fasting; marriages do not normally take place at this time

Liss	Irish fairy fort
Lourdes water	water from holy spring in France which is believed to effect miraculous cures
Malone Road	a wealthy area of Belfast
Mangan	(statue of) 19th-century Irish poet
Mass	church service which consecrates bread and wine in memory of the same action by Jesus before his death
the Mater	hospital in Belfast
maw	gaping mouth
mission	religious group in a foreign country in order to spread their faith
Monastir	a place-name meaning 'monastery;' village near Limerick
mortal sin	a deadly offence, separating the sinner from God
neap (tide)	lowest tide of the year
novena	nine days of prayer for a special petition
offering it up	suffering pain or humiliation for the sake of God
one and six	one-and-a-half shillings
the One with the thin hard foot	the Devil
the only eye in the spud	literally, the only bud on the potato; the only child
the Orange/Orange Lodge/ Orangeman	a society and its members named after Prince William of Orange (also King of England) who led the Protestant troops at the battle of the Boyne in 1690; the colour orange is symbolic of the Northern Protestants
the other sort	derogatory term for Catholics
packman	an old term for a travelling salesman
peat	blocks cut from bogland and dried for fuel
penance	prayers the penitent says after Confession
penitential psalms	long prayers asking for forgiveness of sins
pies	magpies; noisy black-and-white birds
pishrogues	charms or spells

Poor Clares	an order of nuns devoted to the poor
porter	black beer
poteen	illegal alcohol brewed from potatoes
pratie	potato
press	cupboard
Provos	Provisional IRA; a breakaway group from the Irish Republican Army, committed to violence to achieve their aim of independence for the whole of Ireland
putlock oil	oil from scaffolding
Rabelaisian	from Rabelais, the 16th-century French writer renowned for coarse humour and lively, vivid language
Red Sea	the sea in the Bible which parted to let Moses and the Israelites pass; it closed to drown Pharaoh's soldiers
refectarian	nun in charge of the place where meals are eaten
retreat	temporary withdrawal from normal life for religious meditation
Sacred Heart	a statue or picture of Jesus showing His loving heart
St Brigit	female saint, patroness of Ireland and of virgins; feastday on February 1st
sally-rod	thin willow branch used for weaving baskets, etc
Saracen	armoured personnel carrier
scapular	a cloth badge of religious significance
sea-wrack	seaweed
sectarian murder	murder of one member of a community by a member of a different sect, eg Catholics and Protestants
seeney pods	senna pods; a purgative
shamrock	a small, green, three-leafed plant symbolic of Ireland
sidecar	horsedrawn cart with passengers facing out at each side

sitfast and scutch	invasive weeds
sod	square of turf or peat for fuel
soda farl	thin, triangular cake made with soda and buttermilk
Sodalities	religious societies
spring-tide	tide of maximum height in the year
strand	beach
Tans	Black and Tans; force recruited from British ex-soldiers during the War of Independence, so called because of their uniforms; notoriously violent against people and property
tarred and feathered	punishment for informers or collaborators; the victim's head is shaved and hot tar is poured over it, stuck with feathers
Teague	derogatory term for Catholic
Teddy boys	young men of the 1950s with their own version of Edwardian dress
teem out a fulltide	bale out the tide – an impossibility
Tenebrae	(Latin: darkness) Catholic Good Friday service which commemorates the death of Jesus. It takes place in increasing darkness as candles are extinguished; some form of clapper is used instead of bells to denote the beginning and end of prayers
togs	slang for swimming costume; clothes
Tory	a rocky island off the coast of Donegal
tout	informer
Tree of Knowledge/Tree of Good and Evil/ Tree of Life	reference to the Biblical story of how Adam and Eve were tempted by the serpent to eat fruit, traditionally an apple, from the forbidden tree; they did so and were expelled from Paradise
Trinity	God as Father, Son and Holy Spirit
Twelfth of July	commemoration by Protestant loyalists in Northern Ireland of the victory of William of Orange over Catholic forces in 1690; banners with pictures of William of Orange and the

	British monarch are carried round the streets by pipe bands and marchers
unfrocked	a priest who has been dismissed from the priesthood
venial sin	a lesser offence against God
wake	memorial celebration for the dead in the home
wake bed	bed where the dead body lies during the last visit of family and friends
West Briton	insulting term for Anglicised Irish person
W.B. Yeats	Ireland's most famous poet